BIBLE MEMORY

Word Games

2-in-1

BIBLE MEMORY
Word Games
2-in-1

**Featuring Crosswords and Word Searches—
100 Puzzles in All!**

BARBOUR
PUBLISHING

Published by Barbour Publishing, Inc., 1810 Barbour Drive, Uhrichsville, Ohio 44683, www.barbourbooks.com

Our mission is to inspire the world with the life-changing message of the Bible.

Member of the
Evangelical Christian
Publishers Association

Printed in the United States of America.

THE PERFECT MATCH:
Crossword and Word Search Puzzles
Based on Bible Memory Verses!

This collection is sure to satisfy both the passionate word game fan and the avid scripture memorizer. A total of one hundred puzzles—fifty of each type—are drawn entirely from passages of the beloved King James Version.

How do Bible memory word games work? Here are details:

CROSSWORDS

Each puzzle begins with scriptures that include crossword coordinates for several missing words. For example, the missing word where (1D) appears in the scripture will fit into 1 Down on the grid. (4A) means 4 Across, and so forth. Don't know some of the missing words? Try filling in other words in the grid and use the filled-in letters to make a better guess. Entries made up of multiple words include a hint so you know you're looking for more than one word—for example, (3W) means the answer is three words smooshed together in one entry.

WORD SEARCHES

Each puzzle begins with scriptures that include blanks for several words. Fill in the blanks and then find those words in the search grid. Don't know some of the missing words? Try finding the words in the search grid first. Entries made up of multiple words include a hint so you know you're looking for more than one word—for example, (3W) means the answer is three words, and they'll be found end-to-end in the search grid.

Crosswords begin on the next page. Word searches start on page 106. Of course, answers are provided, beginning on page 206.

Are you up for the challenge? Get ready for the heavenly encouragement of scripture and the fun of word games!

Thy word have I hid in mine heart,
that I might not sin against thee.
PSALM 119:11

1. CREATION PART 1

Genesis 1:1-8

In the (7A) God (14D) the heaven and the (10A). **2** And the earth was without form, and (17D); and darkness was upon the face of the (12A). And the (9A) of God moved upon the face of the waters. **3** And God said, (1A) (2D) (7D) light: and there was light. **4** And God saw the light, that (18A) was (20A): and God divided the (6D) from the (5D). **5** And God (19A) the light Day, and the darkness he called (11D). And the evening and the (15A) were the first day. **6** And God said, Let there be a firmament in the midst of the (8D), and let it divide the waters from the waters. **7** And God made the firmament, and (5A) the waters which were under the firmament from the waters which were above the firmament: and it (3A) so. **8** And God called the firmament (16A). And the (13D) and the morning were the (4D) day.

3. CREATION PART 3

Genesis 1:20-25

And God said, Let the waters bring forth abundantly the moving creature that hath (12A), and (11A) that may fly above the (13D) in the open firmament of (9A). **21** And God created great (2D), and every living creature that moveth, which the (10D) brought forth abundantly, after their kind, and every (2A) fowl after his kind: and God saw that it was good. **22** And God (14A) them, saying, Be fruitful, and (7A), and fill the waters in the seas, and let fowl multiply in the earth. **23** And the evening and the morning were the fifth (8A). **24** And God said, Let the earth bring forth the (4A) (3D) after his kind, cattle, and creeping thing, and beast of the earth after his kind: and it was so. **25** And God made the (1D) of the earth after his kind, and (6A) after their kind, and every thing that (3A) upon the earth (15A/3W): and God saw that (5D/3W).

4. CREATION PART 4

Genesis 1:26-29, 31; 2:1-3

And God said, Let us make man in our (1A), after our likeness: and let them have (18A) over the fish of the (5A), and over the fowl of the (2D), and over the (9D), and over all the earth, and over every creeping thing that (3D) upon the (19A). **27** So God created man in his own image, in the (8D) of God created he him; male and female created he them. **28** And God blessed them, and God said unto them, Be (11D), and multiply, and (12A) the earth, and subdue it: and have dominion over the (16D) of the sea, and over the fowl of the air, and over every living thing that moveth upon the earth. **29** And God said, Behold, I have given you every herb bearing (14A), which is upon the face of all the earth, and every tree, in the which is the (17A) of a tree yielding seed; to you it shall be for meat. . . . **31** And God saw every thing that he had made, and, behold, it was very good. And the (10A) and the morning were the (15A) day. . . . **1** Thus the (4D) and the earth were finished, and all the host of them. **2** And on the (13D) day God ended his work which he had made; and he (6A) on the seventh day from all his work which he had made. **3** And God blessed the seventh day, and (7D) it: because that in it he had rested from all his work which God created and made.

5. ADAM

Genesis 2:7-17

And the LORD God (13D) man of the dust of the ground, and breathed into his nostrils the breath of life; and man became a living soul. **8** And the LORD God planted a garden eastward in (12A); and there he put the man whom he had formed. **9** And out of the ground made the LORD God to grow every tree that is pleasant to the sight, and good for (15D); the (6D) of life also in the midst of the garden, and the tree of (9A) of good and evil. **10** And a (8A) went out of Eden to water the garden; and from thence it was parted, and became into (4D) heads. **11** The name of the first is (14D): that is it which compasseth the whole land of (3D), where there is gold; **12** and the gold of that land is good: there is bdellium and the onyx stone. **13** And the name of the second river is (2A): the same is it that compasseth the whole land of Ethiopia. **14** And the name of the third river is (1D): that is it which goeth toward the east of Assyria. And the fourth river is (16A). **15** And the LORD God took the man, and put him into the (18A) of Eden to dress it and to keep it. **16** And the LORD God (7D) the man, saying, Of every tree of the garden thou mayest freely (5A): **17** but of the tree of the knowledge of (17A) and (11A), thou shalt not eat of it: for in the day that thou eatest thereof thou shalt surely (10D).

6. EVE

Genesis 2:18-25

And the Lord God said, It is not good that the man should (16A/2W); I will make him an help meet for him. **19** And out of the ground the Lord God formed every beast of the (12A), and every (8A) of the air; and brought them unto (15D) to see what he would call them: and whatsoever Adam called every living (6A), that was the name thereof. **20** And Adam gave names to all (6D), and to the fowl of the air, and to every beast of the field; but for Adam there was not found an (7A/2W) for him. **21** And the Lord God caused a deep (4D) to fall upon Adam, and he slept: and he took one of his (14D), and closed up the flesh instead thereof; **22** and the rib, which the Lord God had taken from man, made he a woman, and (2A) her unto the man. **23** And Adam said, This is now bone of my (9A), and flesh of my (5D): she shall be called Woman, because she was taken out of Man. **24** Therefore shall a man leave his (13A) and his (1D), and shall cleave unto his (11D): and they shall be (3D/2W). **25** And they were both (10D), the man and his wife, and were not (15A).

7. THE TEMPTATION OF EVE

Genesis 3:1-8

Now the serpent was more subtil than any (3D) of the field which the
LORD God had made. And he said unto the (17A), Yea, hath God said,
Ye shall not eat of every tree of the (5D)? **2** And the woman said unto
the (2D), We may eat of the (15D) of the (12A) of the garden: **3** but
of the fruit of the tree which is in the midst of the garden, God hath
said, Ye shall not (7D) of it, neither shall ye (18A) it, lest ye die. **4** And
the serpent said unto the woman, Ye shall not (6A/2W): **5** for God
doth know that in the day ye eat thereof, then your eyes shall be (19A),
and ye shall be as gods, knowing (14D) and (13D). **6** And when the
woman saw that the tree was good for food, and that it was (10D) to the
eyes, and a tree to be desired to make one (11D), she took of the fruit
thereof, and did eat, and gave also unto her (1A) with her; and he did
eat. **7** And the (13A) of them both were opened, and they knew that they
were (9D); and they sewed (4A) leaves together, and made themselves
aprons. **8** And they heard the voice of the LORD God walking in the
garden in the (16D) of the day: and Adam and his wife hid themselves
from the (8A) of the LORD God amongst the trees of the garden.

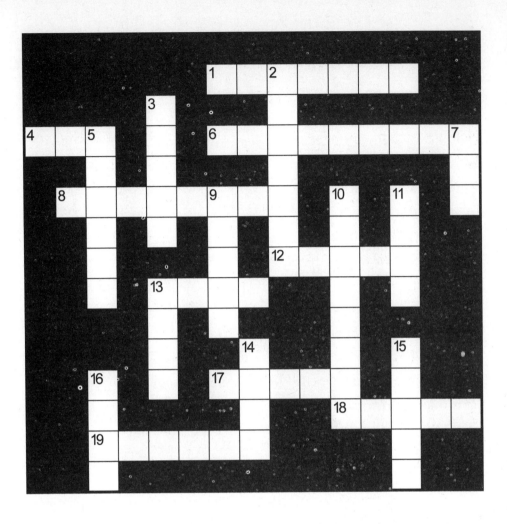

8. NOAH AND THE ARK

Genesis 6:13-22

And God said unto (5D), The end of all flesh is come before me; for the earth is filled with (1D) through them; and, behold, I will (14D) them with the earth. **14** Make thee an ark of (19A/2W); rooms shalt thou make in the ark, and shalt pitch it within and without with pitch. **15** And this is the fashion which thou shalt make it of: The (3D) of the ark shall be three hundred cubits, the (15A) of it fifty (7D), and the (11A) of it thirty cubits. **16** A window shalt thou make to the ark, and in a cubit shalt thou finish it above; and the door of the ark shalt thou set in the side thereof; with lower, second, and (16D) stories shalt thou make it. **17** And, behold, I, even I, do bring a flood of waters upon the earth, to destroy all flesh, wherein is the (9A) of life, from under heaven; and every thing that is in the earth (17A) (14A). **18** But with thee will I establish my (2D); and thou shalt come into the (18D), thou, and thy sons, and thy (4D), and thy sons' wives with thee. **19** And of every (8A) (6D) of all flesh, (13A) of every sort shalt thou bring into the ark, to keep them alive with thee; they shall be male and (12D). **20** Of fowls after their kind, and of cattle after their kind, of every creeping thing of the earth after his kind, two of every sort shall come unto thee, to keep them (10D). **21** And take thou unto thee of all food that is eaten, and thou shalt gather it to thee; and it shall be for food for thee, and for them. **22** Thus did Noah; according to all that God commanded him, so did he.

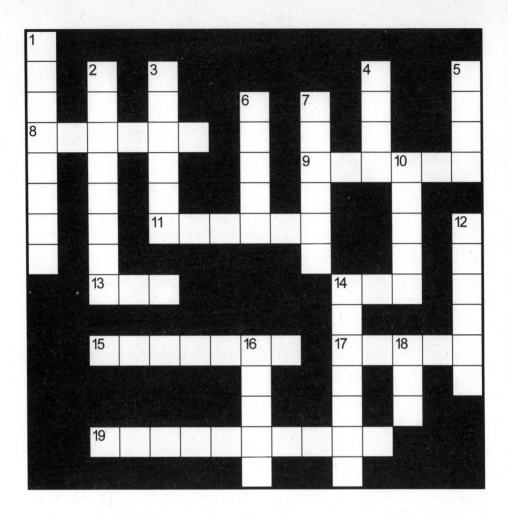

9. THE PROMISE

Genesis 8:1, 15-22

And God remembered (1D), and every living thing, and all the cattle that was with him in the ark. . . . **15** And God (17D) unto Noah, saying, **16** Go forth of the ark, thou, and thy wife, and thy sons, and thy sons' wives with thee. **17** Bring forth with thee every living thing that is with thee, of all flesh, both of fowl, and of cattle, and of every creeping thing that (4D) upon the earth; that they may (9A) abundantly in the earth, and be fruitful, and multiply upon the (8A). **18** And Noah went forth, and his (18D), and his (3D), and his sons' wives with him: **19** every beast, every creeping thing, and every fowl, and whatsoever creepeth upon the earth, after their kinds, went forth (12A) of the (6A). **20** And Noah builded an (15D) unto the LORD; and took of every clean beast, and of every clean fowl, and offered burnt (16A) on the altar. **21** And the LORD smelled a (10A) (19A); and the LORD said in his heart, I will not again (5D) the ground any more for man's sake; for the (2D) of man's heart is evil from his youth; neither will I again (20A) any more every thing living, as I have done. **22** While the earth remaineth, seedtime and (7D), and cold and (14A), and summer and (11D), and day and (13A) shall not cease.

10. GOD'S COVENANT WITH ABRAM

Genesis 12:1-3; 15:18-21

Now the LORD had said unto (5A), Get thee out of thy (10D), and from thy kindred, and from thy father's (7D), unto a land that I will shew thee: **2** and I will make of thee a great (9A), and I will (12D) thee, and make thy name (14A); and thou shalt be a blessing: **3** and I will bless them that bless thee, and (1A) him that (3D) thee: and in thee shall all (2D) of the earth be blessed. . . . **18** In the same day the (11A) made a (1D) with Abram, saying, Unto thy seed have I given this (4D), from the river of Egypt unto the great river, the river (6A): **19** the (13A), and the (8D), and the Kadmonites, **20** and the Hittites, and the Perizzites, and the (15A), **21** and the (5D), and the Canaanites, and the Girgashites, and the Jebusites.

11. ABRAHAM AND ISAAC

Genesis 22:1-2, 6-13

And it (19A) to (12A) after these things, that God did tempt Abraham, and said unto him, Abraham: and he said, Behold, here I am. **2** And he said, Take now thy son, thine only son (3D), whom thou (13D), and get thee into the land of (16A); and offer him there for a burnt offering upon one of the (4A) which I will tell thee of. . . . **6** And Abraham took the wood of the (1D) (9D), and laid it upon Isaac his son; and he took the fire in his hand, and a knife; and they went both of them together. **7** And Isaac spake unto Abraham his father, and said, (4D) (11D): and he said, Here am I, my son. And he said, Behold the fire and the (8A): but where is the lamb for a burnt offering? **8** And Abraham said, My son, God will (12D) himself a lamb for a burnt offering: so they went both of them (10A). **9** And they came to the place which God had told him of; and Abraham built an (15D) there, and laid the wood in order, and bound Isaac his son, and laid him on the altar upon the wood. **10** And Abraham stretched forth his hand, and took the (14D) to slay his son. **11** And the (5A) of the (6D) called unto him out of (17A), and said, Abraham, Abraham: and he said, Here am I. **12** And he said, Lay not thine hand upon the lad, neither do thou any thing unto him: for now I know that thou (18A) God, seeing thou hast not withheld thy son, thine only son from me. **13** And Abraham lifted up his (7D), and looked, and behold behind him a ram caught in a (10D) by his horns: and Abraham went and took the (2D), and offered him up for a burnt offering in the stead of his son.

12. JACOB AND ESAU

Genesis 25:21-34

And Isaac intreated the LORD for his wife, because she was (19A): and the LORD was (20A) of him, and Rebekah his wife conceived. **22** And the children (6A) together within her; and she said, If it be so, why am I thus? And she went to enquire of the LORD. **23** And the LORD said unto her, (13D) (4A) are in thy womb, and two manner of people shall be separated from thy (3D); and the one people shall be (8A) than the other people; and the elder shall serve the younger. **24** And when her days to be delivered were fulfilled, behold, there were (14D) in her womb. **25** And the first came out red, all over like an hairy (7D); and they called his name (9A). **26** And after that came his brother out, and his hand took hold on Esau's (18D); and his name was called (5A): and Isaac was threescore years old when she bare them. **27** And the boys grew: and Esau was a cunning hunter, a man of the field; and Jacob was a plain man, dwelling in (12A). **28** And Isaac loved Esau, because he did eat of his (10D): but (11A) loved Jacob. **29** And Jacob sod pottage: and Esau came from the field, and he was faint: **30** and Esau said to Jacob, (17D) me, I pray thee, with that same red pottage; for I am (16D): therefore was his name called Edom. **31** And Jacob said, Sell me this day thy (15A). **32** And Esau said, Behold, I am at the point to die: and what (2D) shall this birthright do to me? **33** And Jacob said, Swear to me this day; and he sware unto him: and he sold his birthright unto Jacob. **34** Then Jacob gave Esau bread and pottage of (21A); and he did eat and drink, and rose up, and went his way: thus Esau (1A) his birthright.

13. MOSES IN THE BASKET

Exodus 2:1-10

And there went a man of the (9A) of (8D), and took to wife a daughter of Levi. **2** And the woman conceived, and (18D) a son: and when she saw him that he was a (1A) child, she hid him (10A) (15D). **3** And when she could not longer hide him, she took for him an ark of bulrushes, and daubed it with slime and with (16D), and put the child therein; and she laid it in the flags by the river's brink. **4** And his (14D) stood afar off, to wit what would be done to him. **5** And the daughter of (20A) came down to (7D) (6A) at the river; and her maidens walked along by the river's side; and when she saw the ark among the flags, she sent her (12D) to fetch it. **6** And when she had opened it, she saw the (17A): and, behold, the babe wept. And she had compassion on him, and said, This is one of the Hebrews' (19A). **7** Then said his sister to Pharaoh's (3D), Shall I go and call to thee a nurse of the (4D) women, that she may nurse the child for thee? **8** And Pharaoh's daughter said to her, Go. And the maid went and called the child's mother. **9** And Pharaoh's daughter said unto her, Take this child away, and nurse it for me, and I will give thee thy wages. And the women took the child, and (13D) it. **10** And the child (1D), and she brought him unto Pharaoh's daughter, and he (5A) her son. And she called his name Moses: and she said, Because I (2D) (11A) out of the water.

14. MOSES AND THE BURNING BUSH

Exodus 3:1-8

Now Moses kept the flock of Jethro his (1D) in (10A), the priest of (9D): and he led the (5A) to the backside of the desert, and came to the (15A) of God, even to Horeb. **2** And the (13D) of the LORD appeared unto him in a flame of fire out of the midst of a (4D): and he looked, and, behold, the bush burned with (1A), and the bush was not consumed. **3** And (16A) said, I will now turn aside, and see this great sight, why the bush is not burnt. **4** And when the LORD saw that he turned aside to see, God called unto him out of the midst of the bush, and said, Moses, Moses. And he said, Here am I. **5** And he said, Draw not nigh hither: put off thy (2A) from off thy feet, for the place whereon thou standest is (3D) (14D). **6** Moreover he said, I am the God of thy father, the God of (8A), the God of (11A), and the God of (7D). And Moses hid his (17D); for he was afraid to look upon God. **7** And the LORD said, I have surely seen the (18A) of my people which are in (19A), and have heard their cry by reason of their taskmasters; for I know their sorrows; **8** and I am come down to deliver them out of the hand of the Egyptians, and to bring them up out of that land unto a good land and a large, unto a land flowing with milk and (12A); unto the place of the (6D), and the Hittites, and the Amorites, and the Perizzites, and the Hivites, and the Jebusites.

15. THE CROSSING OF THE RED SEA

Exodus 14:21-23, 26-31

And Moses stretched out his hand over the sea; and the LORD caused the sea to go back by a strong (11D) wind all that night, and made the sea (14A) land, and the waters were divided. **22** And the children of Israel went into the midst of the sea upon the dry (8A): and the waters were a wall unto them on their right hand, and on their (19A). **23** And the Egyptians pursued, and went in after them to the midst of the sea, even all Pharaoh's horses, his (3D), and his (18A). . . . **26** And the LORD said unto (16D), Stretch out thine hand over the sea, that the waters may come again upon the (7D), upon their chariots, and upon their horsemen. **27** And Moses stretched forth his hand over the sea, and the sea returned to his strength when the (13D) appeared; and the Egyptians fled against it; and the LORD (2D) the Egyptians in the midst of the sea. **28** And the waters returned, and (5A) the chariots, and the horsemen, and all the host of (9A) that came into the sea after them; there remained not so much as one of them. **29** But the children of (6D) walked upon dry land in the midst of the sea; and the waters were a wall unto them on their (15D) hand, and on their left. **30** Thus the LORD (17A) Israel that day out of the (12D) of the Egyptians; and Israel saw the Egyptians dead upon the (10A/2W). **31** And Israel saw that great work which the LORD did upon the Egyptians: and the people (1D) the LORD, and (4A) the LORD, and his servant Moses.

16. SAMUEL'S CALLING

1 Samuel 3:2-11, 19-21

And it came to pass at that time, when Eli was laid down in his place, and his eyes began to (15A) (4D), that he could not see; **3** and ere the (16D) of God went out in the (18A) of the LORD, where the ark of God was, and Samuel was laid down to sleep; **4** that the LORD called (7A): and he answered, Here am I. **5** And he ran unto Eli, and said, (9D) am I; for thou calledst me. And he said, I called not; lie down again. And he went and (17A) down. **6** And the LORD called yet again, Samuel. And Samuel (5A) and went to Eli, and said, Here am I; for thou didst call me. And he answered, I called not, my son; lie down again. **7** Now Samuel did not yet know the LORD, neither was the word of the LORD yet (10D) unto him. **8** And the LORD called Samuel again the (14A) time. And he arose and went to Eli, and said, Here am I; for thou didst call me. And Eli (3D) that the LORD had called the child. **9** Therefore Eli said unto Samuel, Go, lie down: and it shall be, if he call thee, that thou shalt say, (19A), LORD; for thy (1D) heareth. So Samuel went and lay down in his place. **10** And the LORD came, and stood, and called as at other times, Samuel, Samuel. Then Samuel answered, Speak; for thy servant (6D). **11** And the LORD said to Samuel, Behold, I will do a thing in Israel, at which both the ears of every one that heareth it shall (11D). . . . **19** And Samuel (12A), and the LORD was with him, and did let none of his words fall to the ground. **20** And all Israel from Dan even to (2D) knew that Samuel was established to be a (3A) of the LORD. **21** And the LORD appeared again in (8A): for the LORD revealed himself to Samuel in Shiloh by the (13D) of the (16A).

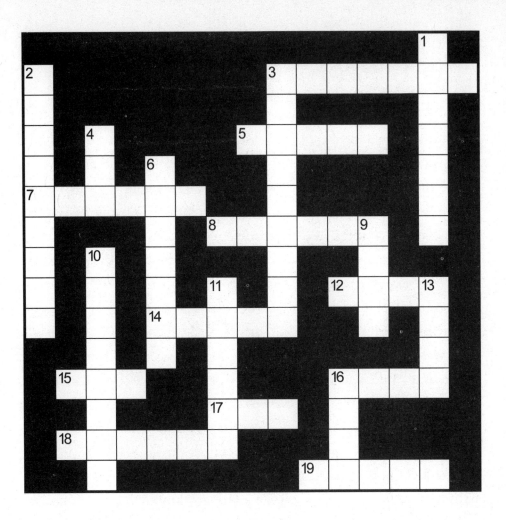

17. DAVID AND GOLIATH

1 Samuel 17:45-51

Then said David to the (4D), Thou comest to me with a (10A), and with a spear, and with a shield: but I come to thee in the name of the LORD of hosts, the God of the armies of (3D), whom thou hast (2A). **46** This day will the LORD (11D) thee into mine hand; and I will (8D) (17A), and take thine head from thee; and I will give the carcases of the host of the Philistines this day unto the fowls of the air, and to the wild beasts of the earth; that all the earth may know that there is a God in Israel. **47** And all this (7A) shall know that the LORD saveth not with sword and (19A): for the battle is the LORD's, and he will give you (1D) our (14D). **48** And it came to pass, when the Philistine arose, and came, and drew nigh to meet David, that David hastened, and ran toward the (15A) to meet the Philistine. **49** And David put his hand in his bag, and took thence a (9A), and slang it, and smote the Philistine in his forehead, that the stone sunk into his (12D); and he fell upon his face to the earth. **50** So David prevailed over the Philistine with a (13A) and with a stone, and smote the Philistine, and slew him; but there was no sword in the hand of David. **51** Therefore David ran, and stood upon the Philistine, and took his sword, and drew it out of the (5A) thereof, and slew him, and (6D/2W) his (18D) therewith. And when the Philistines saw their (16A) was (20A), they fled.

18. DANIEL AND THE LIONS' DEN

Daniel 6:16–23, 28

Then the king commanded, and they brought Daniel, and cast him into the (9A) of (6A). Now the king spake and said unto Daniel, Thy God whom thou servest continually, he will (12D) (13A). **17** And a (2D) was brought, and laid upon the mouth of the den; and the king sealed it with his own (4D), and with the signet of his lords; that the purpose might not be changed concerning Daniel. **18** Then the king went to his (5A), and passed the night (3D): neither were (15A) of musick brought before him: and his sleep went from him. **19** Then the king arose very early in the (10A), and went in haste unto the den of lions. **20** And when he came to the den, he cried with a lamentable voice unto Daniel: and the king spake and said to (14D), O Daniel, servant of the living God, is thy God, whom thou servest continually, able to deliver thee from the lions? **21** Then said Daniel unto the king, O king, (16D) (7D/2W). **22** My God hath sent his angel, and hath shut the lions' (8D), that they have not hurt me: forasmuch as before him innocency was found in me; and also before thee, O king, have I done no hurt. **23** Then was the king (18A) (17D) for him, and commanded that they should take Daniel up out of the den. So Daniel was taken up out of the den, and no manner of hurt was found upon him, because he (11D) in his God. . . . **28** So this Daniel (1A) in the reign of (19A), and in the reign of Cyrus the Persian.

19. THE TOWER OF BABEL

Genesis 11:1-9

And the whole earth was of one (6A), and of one speech. **2** And it (13A) to (9A), as they journeyed from the east, that they found a plain in the land of (11A); and they dwelt there. **3** And they said one to (4D), Go to, let us make (17A), and burn them thoroughly. And they had brick for stone, and slime had they for morter. **4** And they said, Go to, let us (1D) us a city and a (16A), whose top may reach unto (3D); and let us make us a name, lest we be scattered abroad upon the face of the whole (14D). **5** And the LORD came down to see the (7A) and the tower, which the children of (8A) builded. **6** And the LORD said, Behold, the people is one, and they have all one language; and this they begin to do: and now nothing will be restrained from them, which they have (12D) to do. **7** Go to, let us go down, and there (5A) their language, that they may not understand one another's (18A). **8** So the LORD (10D) them abroad from thence upon the (2D) of all the earth: and they left off to build the city. **9** Therefore is the name of it called (1A); because the LORD did there confound the language of all the earth: and from thence did the LORD scatter them (15A) upon the face of all the earth.

20. JACOB'S LADDER

Genesis 28:10-13, 15-16, 18-22

And Jacob went out from (10D), and went toward Haran. 11 And he lighted upon a certain place, and tarried there all night, because the sun was set; and he took of the stones of that place, and put them for his pillows, and lay down in that place to sleep. 12 And he (14D), and behold a (13A) set up on the earth, and the top of it reached to (8D): and behold the (2D) of God ascending and (3A) on it. 13 And, behold, the LORD stood above it, and said, I am the LORD God of (6D) thy father, and the God of (1D): the land whereon thou liest, to thee will I give it, and to thy seed. . . . 15 And, behold, (17A/2W) with (16A), and will keep thee in all places whither thou goest, and will bring thee again into this land; for I will not leave thee, until I have done that which I have spoken to thee of. 16 And (18A) awaked out of his (4D), and he said, Surely the LORD is in this (5A); and I knew it not. . . . 18 And Jacob rose up early in the morning, and took the stone that he had put for his pillows, and set it up for a pillar, and poured oil upon the top of it. 19 And he called the name of that place (11A): but the name of that city was called Luz at the first. 20 And Jacob (19A) a vow, saying, If God will be with me, and will keep me in this way that I go, and will give me (10A) to (7A), and raiment to put on, 21 so that I come again to my father's house in (15D); then shall the LORD (11D/3W): 22 and this stone, which I have set for a (9A), shall be God's house: and of all that thou shalt give me I will surely give the (12D) unto thee.

21. DAVID CHOSEN BY GOD

1 Samuel 16:1, 6–13

And the LORD said unto Samuel, How long wilt thou mourn for Saul, seeing I have rejected him from (7D) over Israel? fill thine (15D) with (14A), and go, I will send thee to Jesse the Bethlehemite: for I have provided me a king among his sons. . . . **6** And it came to pass, when they were come, that he looked on Eliab, and said, Surely the LORD's (11D) is before him. **7** But the LORD said unto (13D), Look not on his countenance, or on the (8D) of his stature; because I have (1D) him: for the LORD seeth not as man seeth; for man looketh on the (4D) appearance, but the LORD looketh on the (5D). **8** Then Jesse called Abinadab, and made him pass before Samuel. And he said, Neither hath the (16A) chosen this. **9** Then Jesse made Shammah to pass by. And he said, Neither hath the LORD (12A) this. **10** Again, Jesse made seven of his (3A) to pass before Samuel. And Samuel said unto Jesse, The LORD hath not chosen these. **11** And Samuel said unto Jesse, Are here all thy (10D)? And he said, There remaineth yet the (17A), and, behold, he keepeth the sheep. And Samuel said unto Jesse, Send and (2A) (5A): for we will not sit down till he come hither. **12** And he sent, and brought him in. Now he was ruddy, and withal of a beautiful (18A), and goodly to look to. And the LORD said, Arise, (9A) him: for this is he. **13** Then Samuel took the horn of oil, and anointed him in the midst of his brethren: and the (6A) of the LORD came upon David from that day forward.

22. THE BATTLE OF JERICHO

Joshua 6:12-16, 20-21

And Joshua rose early in the morning, and the priests took up the ark of the LORD. **13** And seven (13A) bearing (5D) (18A) of rams' horns before the (3D) of the (15A) went on continually, and (6D) with the trumpets: and the armed men went before them; but the rereward came after the ark of the LORD, the priests going on, and (6A) with the trumpets. **14** And the second day they compassed the city once, and returned into the camp: so they did six days. **15** And it came to pass on the (10D) day, that they (4A) early about the dawning of the day, and (1A) the city after the same manner seven times: only on that day they compassed the city seven times. **16** And it came to pass at the seventh time, when the priests blew with the trumpets, (17A) said unto the people, (12D); for the LORD hath given you the city. . . . **20** So the people (14D) when the priests blew with the trumpets: and it (1D) to pass, when the people heard the sound of the trumpet, and the people shouted with a (11D) (16D), that the wall (9D) (2D) (9A), so that the (19A) went up into the city, every man straight before him, and they took the city. **21** And they (7D) (8A) all that was in the city.

23. SHADRACH, MESHACH, AND ABEDNEGO

Daniel 3:14-21, 24-25

Nebuchadnezzar spake and said unto them, Is it true, O Shadrach, Meshach, and Abednego, do not ye serve my gods, nor worship the (9A) (15A) which I have set up? **15** Now if ye be ready that at what time ye hear the sound of the cornet, (8D), harp, sackbut, psaltery, and dulcimer, and all kinds of musick, ye fall down and (17A) the image which I have made; well: but if ye worship not, ye shall be cast the same hour into the midst of a burning (18A) (16A); and who is that God that shall (5D) you out of my hands? **16** (19A), Meshach, and (1D), answered and said to the king, O Nebuchadnezzar, we are not careful to answer thee in this matter. **17** If it be so, our God whom we (10D) is able to deliver us from the burning fiery furnace, and he will deliver us out of thine hand, O king. **18** But if not, be it known unto thee, (2D/2W), that we will not serve thy gods, nor worship the golden image which thou hast set up. **19** Then was Nebuchadnezzar full of fury, and the form of his visage was changed against Shadrach, Meshach, and Abednego: therefore he spake, and commanded that they should heat the furnace one (10A) times more than it was wont to be heated. **20** And he (11D) the most (14D) men that were in his army to bind Shadrach, Meshach, and Abednego, and to cast them into the burning fiery furnace. **21** Then these men were bound in their coats, their hosen, and their hats, and their other (4D), and were cast into the midst of the burning fiery furnace. . . . **24** Then Nebuchadnezzar the king was astonished, and rose up in haste, and spake, and said unto his (12A), Did not we cast (3D) (14A) bound into the midst of the fire? They answered and said unto the king, (6A), O king. **25** He answered and said, Lo, I see four men loose, walking in the midst of the fire, and they have no hurt; and the form of the fourth is like the (13D) of (7A).

24. JOSEPH'S COAT OF MANY COLORS

Genesis 37:3-5, 17-18, 23-24,28, 31-34

Now (2D) loved Joseph more than all his (19A), because he was the son of his old age: and he made him a coat of many colours. **4** And when his brethren saw that their (13D) loved him more than all his brethren, they (17A) (9A), and could not speak (10A) unto him. **5** And Joseph (3D) a dream, and he told it his brethren: and they hated him yet the more. . . . **17** And Joseph went after his (11D), and found them in (7D). **18** And when they saw him afar off, even before he came near unto them, they (5A) against him to slay him. . . . **23** And it came to pass, when (15A) was come unto his brethren, that they stript Joseph out of his coat, his coat of many colours that was on him; **24** and they took him, and cast him (12A) a (6D): and the pit was empty, there was no (8A) in it. . . . **28** Then there passed by Midianites merchantmen; and they drew and lifted up Joseph out of the pit, and sold Joseph to the Ishmeelites for twenty pieces of (1A): and they brought Joseph into (18A). . . . **31** And they took Joseph's coat, and killed a kid of the (14D), and dipped the coat in the blood; **32** and they sent the coat of many colours, and they brought it to their father; and said, This have we found: know now whether it be thy son's coat or no. **33** And he knew it, and said, It is my son's coat; an (16D) beast hath devoured him; Joseph is without doubt rent in pieces. **34** And Jacob rent his clothes, and put sackcloth upon his loins, and (4D) for his son many days.

25. THE GOLDEN CALF

Exodus 32:7-8, 15-20

And the LORD said unto Moses, Go, get thee down; for thy (4D), which thou broughtest out of the land of (1A), have corrupted themselves: **8** they have turned aside quickly out of the way which I (7D) them: they have made them a molten (15D), and have worshipped it, and have sacrificed thereunto, and said, These be thy gods, O Israel, which have brought thee up out of the land of Egypt. . . . **15** And (9A) turned, and went down from the (16A), and the two tables of the (12A) were in his hand: the (2D) were written on both their sides; on the one side and on the other were they (5D). **16** And the tables were the work of God, and the writing was the writing of God, (17A) upon the tables. **17** And when Joshua heard the noise of the people as they shouted, he said unto Moses, There is a (14D) of (5A) in the camp. **18** And he said, It is not the voice of them that shout for mastery, neither is it the voice of them that cry for being (18A): but the noise of them that sing do I hear. **19** And it came to pass, as soon as he came nigh unto the (3A), that he saw the calf, and the (11D): and Moses' anger (10A) hot, and he cast the tables out of his (8D), and brake them beneath the mount. **20** And he took the calf which they had made, and burnt it in the fire, and ground it to (6A), and strawed it upon the water, and made the children of Israel (13A) of it.

26. THE PROMISE OF ISAAC

Genesis 17:1-9, 15-19

And when Abram was ninety years old and nine, the LORD appeared to (2D), and said unto him, I am the (13A) (14D); walk before me, and be thou (8A). **2** And I will make my (5D) between me and thee, and will (7D) thee exceedingly. **3** And Abram fell on his face: and God talked with him, saying, **4** As for me, behold, my covenant is with thee, and thou shalt be a father of many (11D). **5** Neither shall thy name any more be called Abram, but thy name shall be Abraham; for a father of many nations have I made thee. **6** And I will make thee (1D) fruitful, and I will make nations of thee, and (15A) shall come out of thee. **7** And I will establish my covenant (3D) me and thee and thy seed after thee in their generations for an (1A) covenant, to be a God unto thee, and to thy seed after thee. **8** And I will give unto thee, and to thy seed after thee, the land wherein thou art a (6D), all the land of Canaan, for an everlasting possession; and I will be their God. **9** And God said unto Abraham, Thou shalt keep my covenant therefore, thou, and thy seed after thee in their (10A). . . . **15** And God said unto Abraham, As for Sarai thy wife, thou shalt not call her name Sarai, but (4A) shall her name be. **16** And I will bless her, and give thee a son also of her: yea, I will bless her, and she shall be a (12D) of nations; kings of people shall be of her. **17** Then Abraham fell upon his face, and laughed, and said in his heart, Shall a child be born unto him that is an (16A) years old? and shall Sarah, that is ninety years old, bear? **18** And Abraham said unto God, O that Ishmael might live before thee! **19** And God said, Sarah thy wife shall bear thee a son indeed; and thou shalt call his name (9A): and I will establish my covenant with him for an everlasting covenant, and with his seed after him.

27. JACOB WRESTLES WITH THE ANGEL

Genesis 32:22-31

And [Jacob] rose up that (17A), and took his two wives, and his two (2D), and his eleven sons, and passed over the ford Jabbok. **23** And he took them, and sent them over the brook, and sent over that he had. **24** And (4A) was left alone; and there (8D) a man with him until the (11D) of the day. **25** And when he saw that he (15A) not against him, he touched the hollow of his (5A); and the hollow of Jacob's thigh was out of (1D), as he wrestled with him. **26** And he said, (13A/3W), for the day breaketh. And he said, I will not let thee go, except thou (11A) me. **27** And he said unto him, What is thy (12D)? And he said, Jacob. **28** And he said, Thy name shall be called no more Jacob, but (7D): for as a prince hast thou (9A) with God and with (14A), and hast prevailed. **29** And Jacob (10A) him, and said, Tell me, I pray (5D), thy name. And he said, Wherefore is it that thou dost ask after my name? And he blessed him there. **30** And Jacob called the name of the place (6A): for I have seen God face to (3D), and my life is (9D). **31** And as he passed over Penuel the (16A) rose upon him, and he halted upon his thigh.

28. ELIJAH AND BAAL

1 Kings 18:31-39

And Elijah took twelve (2D), according to the number of the tribes of the (10A) of (6D), unto whom the word of the LORD came, saying, Israel shall be thy name: **32** and with the stones he built an (11A) in the name of the LORD: and he made a (14D) about the altar, as great as would contain two measures of seed. **33** And he put the wood in order, and cut the (12A) in pieces, and laid him on the wood, and said, Fill four (5D) with water, and pour it on the burnt (10D), and on the wood. **34** And he said, Do it the second time. And they did it the second time. And he said, Do it the third time. And they did it the (16A) time. **35** And the water ran round about the altar; and he filled the trench also with (19A). **36** And it (1D) to pass at the time of the offering of the evening sacrifice, that (17A) the (13D) came near, and said, LORD God of Abraham, (8A), and of Israel, let it be known this day that thou art God in (4D), and that I am thy (9D), and that I have done all these things at thy word. **37** (18A/2W), O LORD, hear me, that this people may know that thou art the LORD God, and that thou hast turned their heart back again. **38** Then the (3A) of the LORD fell, and consumed the burnt sacrifice, and the wood, and the stones, and the dust, and (15D) up the water that was in the trench. **39** And when all the people saw it, they fell on their (7A): and they said, The LORD, he is the God; the LORD, he is the God.

29. RAHAB AND THE SPIES

Joshua 2:1, 3-4, 6, 15-21

And Joshua the (19D) of (20A) sent out of Shittim two men to (15A) secretly, saying, Go view the land, even (11D). And they went, and came into an harlot's house, named Rahab, and lodged there. . . . **3** And the king of Jericho sent unto Rahab, saying, Bring forth the men that are come to thee, which are entered into thine (16D): for they be come to search out all the (10D). **4** And the woman took the (6D) (9A), and hid them. . . . **6** But she had brought them up to the (17D) of the house, and hid them with the stalks of (3D), which she had laid in order upon the roof. . . . **15** Then she let them down by a cord through the (7A): for her house was upon the town (4A), and she dwelt upon the wall. **16** And she said unto them, Get you to the (12D), lest the pursuers meet you; and hide yourselves there three (13A), until the pursuers be returned: and afterward may ye go your way. **17** And the men said unto her. . . **18** Behold, when we come into the land, thou shalt bind this line of (5A) thread in the window which thou didst let us down by: and thou shalt bring thy (21A), and thy mother, and thy brethren, and all thy father's (14A), home unto thee. **19** And it shall be, that whosoever shall go out of the (18A) of thy house into the street, his (1D) shall be upon his head, and we will be guiltless: and whosoever shall be with thee in the house, his blood shall be on our head, if any hand be upon him. **20** And if thou utter this our (2D), then we will be quit of thine oath which thou hast made us to swear. **21** And she said, According unto your (8D), so be it. And she sent them away, and they departed: and she bound the scarlet line in the window.

30. THE CROSSING OF THE JORDAN

Joshua 3:5, 14-17

And Joshua said unto the people, (9A) yourselves: for to morrow the LORD will do wonders among you. . . . **14** And it (20A) to (6D), when the people removed from their (7A), to pass over Jordan, and the priests bearing the ark of the (11D) before the people; **15** and as they that bare the ark were come unto (16A), and the feet of the (3A) that bare the ark were dipped in the brim of the (12D), (for Jordan overfloweth all his banks all the time of (17A),) **16** that the waters which came down from (13A) stood and rose up upon an heap very far from the city (18D), that is beside Zaretan: and those that came down toward the sea of the plain, even the (14A) (19D), failed, and were cut off: and the people (4D) over right against (5D). **17** And the priests that bare the (10D) of the covenant of the (15D) stood firm on (1D) ground in the midst of Jordan, and all the (2D) passed over on dry ground, until all the people were passed (8A) over Jordan.

31. MANNA AND QUAIL FROM HEAVEN

Exodus 16:4, 11–15

Then said the LORD unto Moses, Behold, I will (13D) bread from (10D) for you; and the people shall go out and gather a certain rate (15A) (17A), that I may prove them, whether they will walk in (14D/2W), or no. . . . 11 And the LORD spake unto (19A), saying, 12 I have heard the (3D) of the children of (12A): speak unto them, saying, At even ye shall eat (11A), and in the morning ye shall be filled with (1A); and ye shall know that I am the (5A) your God. 13 And it (2A) to (6A), that at even the (4D) came up, and covered the camp: and in the morning the dew lay round about the host. 14 And when the (8A) that lay was gone up, (1D), upon the face of the (9D) there lay a small round thing, as small as the hoar frost on the ground. 15 And when the children of Israel saw it, they said one to (18A), It is (7A): for they wist not what it was. And Moses said unto them, This is the bread which the LORD hath given you to (16D).

32. ELIJAH AND THE WIDOW

1 Kings 17:7-16

And it came to pass after a while, that the (19A) dried up, because there had been no rain in the (4D). **8** And the (20A) of the (9A) came unto [Elijah], saying, **9** Arise, get thee to Zarephath, which belongeth to Zidon, and dwell there: behold, I have commanded a (12D) woman there to sustain thee. **10** So he arose and went to Zarephath. And when he came to the gate of the city, behold, the widow woman was there gathering of (11D): and he called to her, and said, Fetch me, I pray thee, a little water in a (15D), that I may (14A). **11** And as she was going to (13A) it, he called to her, and said, Bring me, I pray thee, a morsel of (18D) in thine hand. **12** And she said, As the LORD thy God liveth, I have not a cake, but an (10D) of meal in a barrel, and a little (5D) in a cruse: and, behold, I am gathering two sticks, that I may go in and dress it for me and my son, that we may eat it, and die. **13** And (7D) said unto her, (8A) (1D); go and do as thou hast said: but make me thereof a little (17A) first, and bring it unto me, and after make for thee and for thy son. **14** For thus saith the LORD God of (3D), The (21A) of meal shall not waste, neither shall the (16D) of oil fail, until the day that the LORD sendeth (2A) upon the earth. **15** And she went and did according to the saying of Elijah: and she, and he, and her (10A), did eat many days. **16** And the barrel of meal (6A) not, neither did the cruse of oil fail, according to the word of the LORD, which he spake by Elijah.

33. JONAH

Jonah 2

Then Jonah prayed unto the LORD his God out of the fish's (14A), **2** and said, I cried by reason of mine (10D) unto the LORD, and he heard me; out of the belly of hell cried I, and thou heardest my voice. **3** For thou hadst cast me into the (16A), in the midst of the seas; and the (1D) compassed me about: all thy billows and thy (7D) passed over me. **4** Then I said, I am cast out of thy (8D); yet I will look again toward thy (2D) (13D). **5** The waters compassed me about, even to the soul: the (4D) closed me round about, the (12D) were wrapped about my head. **6** I went down to the bottoms of the (5A); the earth with her bars was about me for ever: yet hast thou brought up my life from corruption, (3A/2W) my God. **7** When my soul fainted within me I remembered the LORD: and my (6A) came in unto thee, into thine holy temple. **8** They that observe lying (15A) forsake their own (20A). **9** But I will sacrifice unto thee with the voice of (9A); I will pay that that I have vowed. (11D) is of the LORD. **10** And the LORD spake unto the fish, and it (17A) out Jonah upon the (18D) (19A).

34. PARABLE OF THE TALENTS

Matthew 25:14-15, 19-29

For the kingdom of heaven is as a man travelling into a far country, who called his own servants, and delivered unto them his goods. **15** And unto one he gave five (4D), to another two, and to another one; to every man according to his several ability; and straightway took his (21A)....**19** After a long time the lord of those servants cometh, and reckoneth with them. **20** And so he that had received five talents came and brought other five talents, saying, (15A), thou deliveredst unto me five talents: behold, I have gained beside them (13A) talents more. **21** His lord said unto him, (19A) (9A), thou good and faithful servant: thou hast been (6D) over a few things, I will make thee ruler over many (10A): enter thou into the joy of thy lord. **22** He also that had received two talents came and said, Lord, thou deliveredst unto me two talents: behold, I have gained two other talents beside them. **23** His lord said unto him, Well done, good and faithful (11D); thou hast been faithful over a few things, I will make thee (16D) over many things: enter thou into the joy of thy (7A). **24** Then he which had (12D) the one talent came and said, Lord, I knew thee that thou art an (3D) man, reaping where thou hast not (1A), and gathering where thou hast not strawed: **25** and I was (18A), and went and hid thy talent in the (20A): lo, there thou hast that is thine. **26** His lord answered and said unto him, Thou (2D) and slothful servant, thou knewest that I reap where I sowed not, and gather where I have not strawed: **27** thou oughtest therefore to have put my (17D) to the exchangers, and then at my coming I should have received mine own with usury. **28** take therefore the talent from him, and give it unto him which hath ten talents. **29** For unto every one that hath shall be given, and he shall have (8A): but from him that hath not shall be (14A) (5A) even that which he hath.

35. PARABLE OF THE SOWER

Matthew 13:3-9, 18-23

Behold, a sower went forth to sow; **4** and when he (11A), some seeds fell by the way side, and the (10D) came and devoured them up: **5** some fell upon (2A) (9A), where they had not much earth: and forthwith they (11D) (8D), because they had no deepness of (13D): **6** and when the sun was up, they were (4D); and because they had no root, they withered away. **7** And some fell among thorns; and the thorns sprung up, and (1D) them: **8** but other fell into good ground, and brought forth (10A), some an hundredfold, some sixtyfold, some thirtyfold. **9** Who hath ears to hear, let him hear. . . . **18** Hear ye therefore the parable of the sower. **19** When any one heareth the word of the (16A), and understandeth it not, then cometh the (12A) (6D), and catcheth away that which was sown in his heart. This is he which received (4A) by the way side. **20** But he that received the seed into stony places, the same is he that heareth the word, and anon with (15D) receiveth it; **21** yet hath he not (17A) in himself, but dureth for a while: for when (3D) or persecution ariseth because of the word, by and by he is (7A). **22** He also that received seed among the thorns is he that heareth the word; and the care of this world, and the deceitfulness of (5A), choke the word, and he becometh (14A). **23** But he that received seed into the good ground is he that heareth the word, and understandeth it; which also beareth fruit, and bringeth forth, some an hundredfold, some sixty, some thirty.

36. PARABLE OF THE PRODIGAL SON

Luke 15:11-24

And he said, A certain man had (21A) (5D): **12** and the younger of them said to his father, Father, give me the portion of goods that falleth to me. And he divided unto them his living. **13** And not many days after the (7A) son gathered all together, and took his (9D) into a far country, and there wasted his substance with (4D) (16D). **14** And when he had spent all, there arose a mighty (19A) in that land; and he began to be in (18D). **15** And he went and joined himself to a citizen of that country; and he sent him into his fields to feed (20A). **16** And he would fain have filled his (15A) with the husks that the swine did eat: and no man gave unto him. **17** And when he came to himself, he said, How many hired (12A) of my father's have bread enough and to spare, and I perish with (11A)! **18** I will arise and go to my father, and will say unto him, Father, I have (10A) against (1D), and before thee, **19** and am no more worthy to be called thy son: make me as one of thy (11D) servants. **20** And he arose, and came to his father. But when he was yet a great way off, his father saw him, and had compassion, and ran, and fell on his neck, and (6D) him. **21** And the son said unto him, Father, I have sinned against heaven, and in thy sight, and am no more worthy to be (3A) (13D/2W). **22** But the father said to his servants, Bring forth the best (2D), and put it on him; and put a (8D) on his hand, and shoes on his (17D): **23** and bring hither the fatted calf, and kill it; and let us eat, and be (14A): **24** for this my son was dead, and is alive again; he was lost, and is found. And they began to be merry.

37. JESUS HEALS MANY

Luke 8:43-48; 17:11-19

And a woman having an issue of (15A) twelve years, which had spent all her living upon physicians, neither could be healed of any, **44** came behind him, and touched the border of his (10A): and immediately her issue of blood stanched. **45** And Jesus said, (6D) (16A) (12A)? When all denied, Peter and they that were with him said, (11D), the multitude throng thee and press thee, and sayest thou, Who touched me? **46** And Jesus said, Somebody hath touched me: for I perceive that (14D) is gone out of me. **47** And when the woman saw that she was not hid, she came (1A), and falling down before him, she declared unto him before all the people for what cause she had touched him, and how she was (9D) immediately. **48** And he said unto her, (17A), be of good comfort: thy faith hath made thee whole; go in peace. . . . **11** And it came to pass, as he went to Jerusalem, that he passed through the midst of Samaria and (3D). **12** And as he entered into a certain village, there met him ten men that were (8A), which stood afar off: **13** and they lifted up their (4D), and said, Jesus, Master, have (2D) on us. **14** And when he saw them, he said unto them, Go shew yourselves unto the (5D). And it came to pass, that, as they went, they were (13D). **15** And one of them, when he saw that he was healed, turned back, and with a loud voice glorified God, **16** and fell down on his face at his feet, giving him thanks: and he was a Samaritan. **17** And Jesus answering said, Were there not ten cleansed? but where are the (19A)? **18** There are not found that returned to give (7A) to God, save this (18A). **19** And he said unto him, Arise, go thy way: thy faith hath made thee (6A).

38. THE HOLY SPIRIT ARRIVES

Acts 2:1-8, 12-21

And when the day of Pentecost was fully come, they were all with one accord in one place. **2** And suddenly there came a sound from heaven as of a rushing (7D) (17D), and it filled all the house where they were sitting. **3** And there appeared unto them cloven tongues like as of (18A), and it sat upon each of them. **4** And they were all filled with the (14A) (10A), and began to speak with other (11D), as the Spirit gave them utterance. **5** And there were dwelling at Jerusalem Jews, devout men, out of every nation under (14D). **6** Now when this was noised abroad, the multitude came together, and were confounded, because that every man heard them speak in his own (15A). **7** And they were all amazed and marvelled, saying one to another, Behold, are not all these which speak Galilaeans? **8** And how hear we every man in our own tongue, wherein we were (19A)? ... **12** And they were all amazed, and were in (2D), saying one to another, What meaneth this? **13** Others mocking said, These men are full of new wine. **14** But Peter, standing up with the (12D), lifted up his voice, and said unto them, Ye men of (1D), and all ye that dwell at Jerusalem, be this known unto you, and hearken to my words: **15** for these are not (5A), as ye suppose, seeing it is but the third hour of the day. **16** But this is that which was spoken by the prophet Joel; **17** And it shall come to pass in the (13D) (3A), saith God, I will pour out of my (8A) upon all flesh: and your sons and your daughters shall prophesy, and your young men shall see visions, and your old men shall dream (3D): **18** and on my servants and on my handmaidens I will pour out in those days of my Spirit; and they shall prophesy: **19** and I will shew wonders in heaven above, and signs in the earth beneath; (4D), and fire, and vapour of (6A): **20** the sun shall be turned into darkness, and the (9D) into blood, before the great and notable day of the Lord come: **21** and it shall come to pass, that whosoever shall call on the name of the Lord shall (16A) (6D).

39. JESUS' BIRTH

Luke 2:1-20

And it came to pass in those days, that there went out a (19A) from Caesar Augustus that all the world should be taxed. **2** (And this taxing was first made when Cyrenius was governor of Syria.) **3** And all went to be (18A), every one into his own city. **4** And (16D) also went up from Galilee, out of the city of (14A), into Judaea, unto the city of David, which is called Bethlehem; (because he was of the house and lineage of (4A):) **5** to be taxed with Mary his espoused wife, being great with (7D). **6** And so it was, that, while they were there, the days were accomplished that she should be delivered. **7** And she brought forth her (1A) son, and wrapped him in swaddling clothes, and laid him in a (10D); because there was no room for them in the inn. **8** And there were in the same country shepherds abiding in the field, keeping watch over their (11A) by night. **9** And, lo, the angel of the Lord came upon them, and the glory of the Lord shone round about them: and they were sore (15D). **10** And the angel said unto them, (6A) (17A): for, behold, I bring you good tidings of great joy, which shall be to all (13D). **11** For unto you is born this day in the city of David a (2D), which is Christ the Lord. **12** And this shall be a sign unto you; Ye shall find the babe wrapped in swaddling (12D), lying in a manger. **13** And suddenly there was with the angel a multitude of the heavenly (9A) praising God, and saying, **14** (8A) to God in the highest, and on earth peace, good will toward men. **15** And it came to pass, as the angels were gone away from them into heaven, the shepherds said one to another, Let us now go even unto (5D), and see this thing which is come to pass, which the Lord hath made known unto us. **16** And they came with haste, and found (10A), and Joseph, and the babe lying in a manger. **17** And when they had seen it, they made known abroad the saying which was told them concerning this child. **18** And all they that heard it wondered at those things which were told them by the

shepherds. **19** But Mary kept all these things, and pondered them in her (3D). **20** And the shepherds returned, glorifying and praising (20D) for all the things that they had heard and seen, as it was (21A) unto them.

40. JESUS DEDICATED AT THE TEMPLE

Luke 2:25-39

And, behold, there was a man in Jerusalem, whose name was (15A); and the same man was just and (13D), waiting for the consolation of Israel: and the (14A) (4A) was upon him. **26** And it was revealed unto him by the Holy Ghost, that he should not see death, before he had seen the Lord's (5A). **27** And he came by the Spirit into the temple: and when the (11D) brought in the child Jesus, to do for him after the custom of the (8A), **28** then took he him up in his arms, and blessed God, and said, **29** Lord, now lettest thou thy servant depart in peace, according to thy word: **30** for mine eyes have seen thy (6D), **31** which thou hast prepared before the face of all people; **32** a light to lighten the Gentiles, and the glory of thy people (3D). **33** And Joseph and his mother marvelled at those things which were spoken of him. **34** And Simeon blessed them, and said unto (10A) his mother, Behold, this (5D) is set for the fall and rising again of many in Israel; and for a sign which shall be spoken against; **35** (yea, a sword shall pierce through thy own (1D) also,) that the thoughts of many hearts may be (9A). **36** And there was one Anna, a prophetess, the daughter of Phanuel, of the tribe of Aser: she was of a great age, and had lived with an (12A) seven years from her virginity; **37** and she was a (2A) of about fourscore and four years, which departed not from the (17A), but served God with fastings and (16A) night and day. **38** And she coming in that instant gave (7D) likewise unto the Lord, and spake of him to all them that looked for redemption in Jerusalem. **39** And when they had performed all things according to the law of the Lord, they returned into (4D), to their own city Nazareth.

41. THE WISE MEN

Matthew 2:1-12

Now when Jesus was born in Bethlehem of Judaea in the days of (20A) the king, behold, there came wise men from the east to Jerusalem, **2** saying, Where is he that is born (13D) of the (17D)? for we have seen his (4D) in the (7A), and are come to worship him. **3** When Herod the king had heard these things, he was (1D), and all Jerusalem with him. **4** And when he had gathered all the chief (11D) and scribes of the people together, he demanded of them where (21A) should be born. **5** And they said unto him, In Bethlehem of Judaea: for thus it is written by the (8A), **6** And thou Bethlehem, in the land of Juda, art not the least among the (9D) of Juda: for out of thee shall come a Governor, that shall (6D) my people Israel. **7** Then Herod, when he had privily called the (14A) (3D), enquired of them diligently what time the star appeared. **8** And he sent them to Bethlehem, and said, Go and search diligently for the young child; and when ye have found him, bring me word again, that I may come and (15D) him also. **9** When they had heard the king, they departed; and, lo, the star, which they saw in the east, went before them, till it came and stood over where the (18A) child was. **10** When they saw the star, they (12A) with exceeding great joy. **11** And when they were come into the (16D), they saw the young child with Mary his mother, and fell down, and worshipped him: and when they had opened their (19A), they presented unto him gifts; (10A), and frankincense and (5A). **12** And being warned of God in a (2A) that they should not return to Herod, they departed into their own country another way.

42. YOUNG JESUS TEACHES AT THE TEMPLE

Luke 2:40-52

And the child (17A), and waxed strong in spirit, filled with (15A): and the grace of God was upon him. **41** Now his (7D) went to Jerusalem every year at the feast of the passover. **42** And when he was (2D) years old, they went up to Jerusalem after the custom of the feast. **43** And when they had fulfilled the days, as they returned, the child Jesus tarried behind in Jerusalem; and (14D) and his mother knew not of it. **44** But they, supposing him to have been in the company, went a day's journey; and they sought him among their kinsfolk and acquaintance. **45** And when they found him not, they turned back again to (10D), seeking him. **46** And it (8A) to (18A), that after three days they found him in the (12A), sitting in the midst of the doctors, both hearing them, and asking them questions. **47** And all that heard him were astonished at his (3D) and answers. **48** And when they saw him, they were (13D): and his mother said unto him, (9A), why hast thou thus dealt with us? behold, thy (1A) and I have sought thee sorrowing. **49** And he said unto them, How is it that ye sought me? wist ye not that I must be about my Father's (11D)? **50** And they understood not the saying which he spake unto them. **51** And he went down with them, and came to Nazareth, and was subject unto them: but his (6A) kept all these sayings in her (5A). **52** And Jesus increased in wisdom and (16A), and in favour with God and (4A).

43. JESUS TURNS WATER INTO WINE

John 2:1-11

And the third day there was a (1A) in Cana of Galilee; and the mother of Jesus was there: **2** and both (16A) was called, and his disciples, to the marriage. **3** And when they wanted (12D), the (13D) of Jesus saith unto him, They have no wine. **4** Jesus saith unto her, (12A), what have I to do with thee? mine hour is not yet come. **5** His mother saith unto the servants, Whatsoever he saith unto you, (5A/2W). **6** And there were set there (9A) waterpots of (15A), after the manner of the purifying of the Jews, containing two or three firkins apiece. **7** Jesus saith unto them, Fill the waterpots with (10A). And they filled them up to the (3D). **8** And he saith unto them, Draw out now, and bear unto the governor of the (4D). And they bare it. **9** When the (11A) of the feast had tasted the water that was made wine, and knew not whence it was: (but the (9D) which drew the water knew;) the (2D) of the feast called the bridegroom, **10** and saith unto him, Every man at the beginning doth set forth good wine; and when men have well (8D), then that which is worse: but thou hast kept the (7A) wine until now. **11** This beginning of (6A) did Jesus in (14A) of Galilee, and manifested forth his (7D); and his disciples (3A) on him.

44. JESUS CALLS SIMON PETER

Luke 5:1-11

And it came to pass, that, as the people pressed upon him to hear the (3D) of (13A), he stood by the lake of Gennesaret, 2 and saw two (10A) standing by the lake: but the fishermen were gone out of them, and were washing their (1A). 3 And he entered into one of the ships, which was Simon's, and prayed him that he would thrust out a little from the land. And he sat down, and (8A) the people out of the ship. 4 Now when he had left speaking, he said unto (2D), Launch out into the (18A), and let down your nets for a draught. 5 And Simon answering said unto him, (12D), we have toiled all the night, and have taken (7D): nevertheless at thy word I will let down the net. 6 And when they had this done, they inclosed a great multitude of (5D): and their net brake. 7 And they beckoned unto their partners, which were in the other ship, that they should come and help them. And they came, and (4D) both the ships, so that they began to (9A). 8 When Simon (11D) saw it, he fell down at Jesus' knees, saying, Depart from me; for I am a sinful man, (14D/2W). 9 For he was astonished, and all that were with him, at the draught of the fishes which they had taken: 10 and so was also James, and (16A), the sons of Zebedee, which were partners with Simon. And (15A) said unto Simon, (4A) not; from henceforth thou shalt catch (17A). 11 And when they had brought their ships to (6A), they forsook all, and (5A) him.

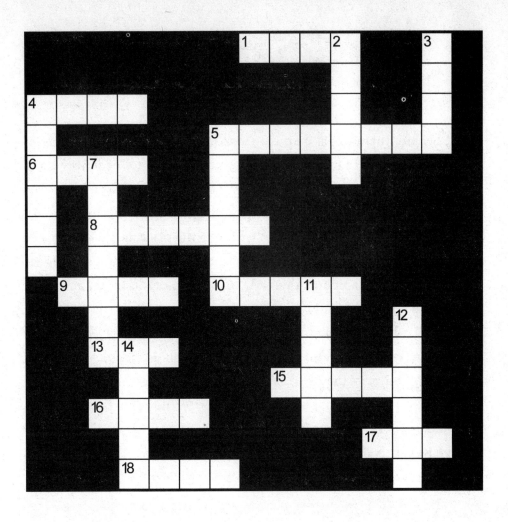

45. ZACCHAEUS

Luke 19:2-10

And, behold, there was a man named Zacchaeus, which was the (15A) among the (8D), and he was (18D). **3** And he sought to see Jesus who he was; and could not for the press, because he was (3D) of stature. **4** And he ran before, and climbed up into a (14D) tree to see him: for he was to pass that way. **5** And when (10A) came to the place, he looked up, and saw him, and said unto him, Zacchaeus, make (16D), and come down; for to day I must abide at thy (7A). **6** And he made haste, and came down, and received him (10D). **7** And when they saw it, they all (1D), saying, That he was gone to be guest with a man that is a (4A). **8** And Zacchaeus stood, and said unto the Lord: Behold, Lord, the half of my (13A) I give to the (9D); and if I have taken any thing from any man by (2D) accusation, I restore him (2A). **9** And Jesus said unto him, This day is (11D) come to this house, forsomuch as he also is a (6D) of (17A). **10** For the Son of man is come to (19A) and to (12D) that which was (5A).

46. PAUL AND SILAS IN PRISON

Acts 16:25-36

And at (2D) Paul and Silas prayed, and (14A) praises unto God: and the prisoners heard them. **26** And suddenly there was a great (3D), so that the foundations of the prison were shaken: and immediately all the (15D) were opened, and every one's bands were loosed. **27** And the keeper of the (20A) awaking out of his (4A), and seeing the prison doors (16D), he drew out his (1D), and would have killed himself, supposing that the (5D) had been fled. **28** But Paul cried with a (6A) voice, saying, Do thyself no (17D): for we are all here. **29** Then he called for a light, and sprang in, and came (7A), and fell down before Paul and Silas, **30** and brought them out, and said, Sirs, what must I do to be (11A)? **31** And they said, Believe on the Lord Jesus Christ, and thou shalt be saved, and thy (9A). **32** And they spake unto him the word of the Lord, and to all that were in his house. **33** And he took them the same hour of the (12D), and washed their stripes; and was (10D), he and all his, straightway. **34** And when he had brought them into his house, he set (18A) before them, and rejoiced, believing in (8D) with all his house. **35** And when it was day, the magistrates sent the serjeants, saying, Let those men go. **36** And the (13D) of the prison told this saying to Paul, The magistrates have sent to let you go: now therefore depart, and go in (19A).

47. JESUS RAISES LAZARUS FROM THE DEAD

John 11:20-27, 32-35, 41-44

Then Martha, as soon as she heard that Jesus was coming, went and met him: but Mary sat still in the house. **21** Then said (14D) unto Jesus, Lord, if thou hadst been here, my brother had not died. **22** But I know, that even now, whatsoever thou wilt ask of (1D), God will give it thee. **23** Jesus saith unto her, Thy (9A) shall rise again. **24** Martha saith unto him, I know that he shall (16A) again in the resurrection at the last (15D). **25** Jesus said unto her, I am the (2D), and the life: he that believeth in me, though he were (15A), yet shall he live: **26** and whosoever liveth and believeth in me shall never die. Believest thou this? **27** She saith unto him, Yea, Lord: I believe that thou art the (17A), the Son of God, which should come into the (4D). . . . **32** Then when Mary was come where Jesus was, and saw him, she fell down at his (10A), saying unto him, Lord, if thou hadst been here, my brother had not (3A). **33** When Jesus therefore saw her weeping, and the (11A) also (13D) which came with her, he groaned in the (12D), and was troubled. **34** And said, Where have ye laid him? They said unto him, Lord, come and see. **35** Jesus (13A). . . . **41** Then they took away the (8D) from the place where the dead was laid. And Jesus lifted up his eyes, and said, Father, I thank thee that thou hast (5D) me. **42** And I knew that thou hearest me always: but because of the people which stand by I said it, that they may believe that thou hast sent me. **43** And when he thus had spoken, he cried with a loud voice, (7A), come forth. **44** And he that was dead came forth, bound (5A) and foot with graveclothes: and his face was bound about with a napkin. Jesus saith unto them, (6A) him, and let him go.

48. THE WOMAN AT THE WELL

John 4:5-7, 9-11, 13-19, 25-26, 28-30

Then cometh [Jesus] to a city of Samaria. . . . **6** Now Jacob's well was there. (6A) therefore, being wearied with his journey, sat thus on the well: and it was about the sixth hour. **7** There cometh a (2A) of Samaria to draw (8A): Jesus saith unto her, Give me to drink. . . . **9** Then saith the woman of (16A) unto him, How is it that thou, being a (6D), askest drink of me, which am a woman of Samaria? for the Jews have no dealings with the Samaritans. **10** Jesus answered and said unto her, If thou knewest the (5A) of (17A), and who it is that saith to thee, Give me to drink; thou wouldest have asked of him, and he would have given thee (1D) water. **11** The woman saith unto him, Sir, thou hast nothing to (11D) with, and the well is deep: from whence then hast thou that living water? . . . **13** Jesus answered and said unto her, Whosoever drinketh of this water shall thirst again: **14** but whosoever drinketh of the water that I shall give him shall never (15D); but the water that I shall give him shall be in him a (14A) of water springing up into everlasting (4D). **15** The woman saith unto him, Sir, give me this water, that I thirst not, neither come hither to draw. **16** Jesus saith unto her, Go, call thy (13D), and come hither. **17** The woman (3D) and said, I have no husband. Jesus said unto her, Thou hast well said, I have no husband: **18** for thou hast had (7A) husbands; and he whom thou now hast is not thy husband: in that saidst thou (10D). **19** The woman saith unto him, Sir, I perceive that thou art a (12A). . . . **25** I know that Messias cometh, which is called (9A): when he is come, he will tell us all things. **26** Jesus saith unto her, I that speak unto thee am he. . . . **28** The woman then left her (18A), and went her way into the (9D), and saith to the men, **29** Come, see a man, which told me all things that ever I did: is not this the Christ? **30** Then they went out of the city, and came unto him.

49. JESUS CALMS THE STORM

Mark 4:35-41

And the same (14A), when the even was come, he saith unto them, Let us pass over unto the other (1D). **36** And when they had sent away the (8D), they took him even as he was in the (16D). And there were also with him other (2D) ships. **37** And there arose a great (7A) of wind, and the (3D) beat into the ship, so that it was now (17A). **38** And he was in the hinder part of the ship, asleep on a (13D): and they awake him, and say unto him, (19A), carest thou not that we (18A)? **39** And he arose, and rebuked the (3A), and said unto the sea, (6A), be (1A). And the wind ceased, and there was a great (5A). **40** And he (4D) unto them, Why are ye so (9D)? how is it that ye have no (12D)? **41** And they feared exceedingly, and said one to (15A), What (11D) of man is this, that even the wind and the (10A) obey him?

50. PETER WALKS ON WATER

Matthew 14:22-33

And straightway Jesus constrained his (7D) to get into a ship, and to go before him unto the other side, while he sent the multitudes away. **23** And when he had sent the multitudes away, he went up into a mountain apart to (14D): and when the evening was come, he was there (15A). **24** But the ship was now in the midst of the (1A), tossed with (2D): for the wind was contrary. **25** And in the fourth watch of the (18D) Jesus went unto them, walking on the sea. **26** And when the disciples saw him walking on the sea, they were troubled, saying, It is a (11A); and they cried out for (10D). **27** But straightway Jesus spake unto them, saying, Be of good (21A); it is I; be not (19A). **28** And Peter answered him and said, Lord, if it be thou, bid me come unto thee on the (16D). **29** And he said, Come. And when (22A) was come down out of the (1D), he walked on the water, to go to (9A). **30** But when he saw the wind boisterous, he was afraid; and beginning to (17A), he cried, saying, Lord, (5A) (3D). **31** And immediately Jesus stretched forth his (13D), and caught him, and said unto him, O thou of little (12A), wherefore didst thou (8D)? **32** And when they were come into the ship, the wind ceased. **33** Then they that were in the ship came and (6A) him, saying, Of a truth thou art the (4D) of (20A).

1. CREATION PART 1

Genesis 1:1-8

In the __ __ __ __ __ __ __ __ __ God

__ __ __ __ __ __ __ the heaven and the

__ __ __ __ __. 2 And the earth was without form,

and __ __ __ __; and darkness was upon the face of

the __ __ __ __. And the __ __ __ __ __ __ of

God moved upon the __ __ __ __ of the waters. 3 And

God said, __ __ __   __ __ __ __ __   __ __

__ __ __ __ __ (4w): and there was light. 4 And God saw the

light, that __ __   __ __ __ __   __ __ __ __ (3w): and

God divided the light from the __ __ __ __ __ __ __ __ __.

5 And God __ __ __ __ __ __ the light __ __ __, and the

darkness he called __ __ __ __ __. And the evening and the

__ __ __ __ __ __ __ were the first day. 6 And God said, Let

there be a __ __ __ __ __ __ __ __ __ in the midst of the

waters, and let it divide the waters from the __ __ __ __ __ __.

7 And God made the firmament, and __ __ __ __ __ __ __

the waters which were under the firmament from the

waters which were above the firmament: and __ __

__ __ __   __ __ (3w). 8 And God called the firmament

__ __ __ __ __ __. And the __ __ __ __ __ __ __ and

the morning were the __ __ __ __ __ __   __ __ __ (2w).

```
G Y I T R D O O G S A W T I T
W E H C O R I E T P I O H T D
B F A O E Y T O C I T N G W B
D A Y N I G H T V R I E I A N
E V E N I N G U B I O C L S S
H Y O S T I T G N T U A E S A
A A I N G N I N N I G E B O T
L D H O L R O K G O C G E E S
X D L E N O Q B D A R N R I S
T N E M A M R I F W E E E M E
N O N E A V V B D K A K H A N
E C A I W I E E L R T G T N K
R E W O D N Y N T O E N T S R
G S R E T A W H N Y D E E P A
Q E D U O Y N H E C A L L E D
```

2. CREATION PART 2

Genesis 1:9-19

And God said, Let the waters under the __ __ __ __ __ __
be gathered together unto one place, and let the __ __ __
__ __ __ __ (2w) appear: and it was so. **10** And God called
the dry land __ __ __ __ __; and the gathering together of
the waters called he __ __ __ __: and God saw that it was
good. **11** And God said, Let the earth bring forth grass, the herb
yielding seed, and the __ __ __ __ __ __ __ __ __ (2w)
yielding fruit after his kind, whose seed is in itself, upon the
earth: and __ __ __ __ __ __ __ (3w). **12** And the
earth __ __ __ __ __ __ __ __ __ __ __ (2w)
grass, and herb yielding seed after his kind, and the tree
__ __ __ __ __ __ __ __ fruit, whose __ __ __ __
was in itself, after __ __ __ __ __ __ __ (2w): and God
saw that it was good. **13** And the __ __ __ __ __ __ __
and the morning were the third day. **14** And God said, __ __ __
__ __ __ __ __ __ __ (3w) lights in the firmament of
the heaven to divide the day from the __ __ __ __ __; and
let them be for signs, and for __ __ __ __ __ __ __, and
for days, and years: **15** and let them be for lights in the firmament
of the heaven to give light upon the earth: and it was so. **16** And
God made two great lights; the greater light to __ __ __ __
__ __ __ __ __ __ (3w), and the lesser __ __ __ __ __
to rule the night: he made the __ __ __ __ __ also. **17** And
God set them in the firmament of the heaven to give light upon the
earth, **18** and to rule over the day and over the night, and to divide
the light from the __ __ __ __ __ __ __ __: and God saw
that it was good. **19** And the evening and the morning were the
__ __ __ __ __ __ day.

```
S Y M I A S E A S O N S F D E
E U M O O D T I O N P S I T A
N T I A K G N I N E V E L A L
O E N W T H E A V E N N I O T
R N I E R S B K L T N K N E L
H L H L S A E S S Y A R U Y N
F R U I T T R E E C R A A I C
O H R T A Q E Q U A V D G E K
U A E W R U H T R A E H T L S
R T Y A S O T S I H T W E D E
T C B S R R T L T L S E S I E
H A K S E B E E H I S K I N D
B E E O O L L D O G Y J U G D
L H T M N U M I N H N T N E M
L G A B R O U G H T F O R T H
```

3. CREATION PART 3

Genesis 1:20-25

And __ __ __ __ __ __ __ (2w), Let the waters bring forth abundantly the moving creature that hath __ __ __ __, and __ __ __ __ that may fly above the __ __ __ __ __ in the open firmament of __ __ __ __ __ __. **21** And God created great __ __ __ __ __ __, and every living creature that moveth, which the __ __ __ __ __ __ brought forth __ __ __ __ __ __ __ __ __ __ __, after their kind, and every __ __ __ __ __ __ fowl after his kind: and God saw that it was good. **22** And God __ __ __ __ __ __ __ them, saying, Be fruitful, and __ __ __ __ __ __ __ __, and __ __ __ __ __ __ __ __ __ __ __ __ (3w) in the seas, and let fowl multiply in the earth. **23** And the evening and the __ __ __ __ __ __ __ were the fifth __ __ __. **24** And God said, Let the earth bring forth the __ __ __ __ __ __ __ __ __ __ __ __ __ (2w) after his kind, cattle, and creeping thing, and beast of the earth after his kind: and it was so. **25** And God made the __ __ __ __ __ of the earth after his kind, and __ __ __ __ __ __ after their kind, and every thing that __ __ __ __ __ __ __ __ upon the earth __ __ __ __ __ __ __ __ __ __ __ __ (3w): and God saw that __ __ __ __ __ __ __ __ (3w).

```
A N C N A L D I A S D O G S A
B L E S S E D D O B M K E E N
U Y O Y G Y L E N W A T E R S
N H A N L N E V A E H N S U O
D N I K S I H R E T F A T T M
A W O I T W A S G O O D L A A
N M G B N X E H K L T Y A E W
T U F I L L T H E W A T E R S
L L Y V C R N H E O L K H C Y
Y T R E A R S T O F O T W G I
W I H E T A H T M O R N I N G
R P G H T R S E F R W E C I R
V L K L L A A I R S O N F V A
D Y A D E H R M E P U Q K I Z
N I N B D C R E E P E T H L L
```

4. CREATION PART 4

Genesis 1:26-29, 31; 2:1-3

And God said, Let us make man in our __ __ __ __ __,
after our likeness: and let them have __ __ __ __ __ __ __ __
over the fish __ __ __ __ __ __ __ __ (3w), and over
the fowl __ __ __ __ __ __ __ __ (3w), and over the
__ __ __ __ __ __, and over all the earth, and over every
creeping thing that __ __ __ __ __ __ __ __ upon the
__ __ __ __ __. **27** So God created man in his own image,
in the __ __ __ __ __ __ __ __ __ __ (3w)
created he him; male and female __ __ __ __ __ __ __ __
he them. **28** And God blessed them, and God said unto them,
Be __ __ __ __ __ __ __ __, and multiply, and
__ __ __ __ __ __ __ __ __ the earth, and subdue
it: and have dominion over the __ __ __ __ of the sea, and
over the fowl of the air, and over every living thing that moveth
upon the earth. **29** And God said, Behold, I have given you every
herb bearing __ __ __ __, which is upon the face of all the
earth, and every tree, in the which is the __ __ __ __ __ of
a tree yielding seed; to you it shall be for meat. . . . **31** And God
saw every thing that he had made, and, behold, it was very good.
And the __ __ __ __ __ __ __ and the morning were the
__ __ __ __ __ day. . . . **1** Thus the __ __ __ __ __ __ __
and the earth were finished, and all the host of them. **2** And on the
__ __ __ __ __ __ __ day God ended his work which he had
made; and he __ __ __ __ __ __ on the seventh day from all
his work which he had made. **3** And God blessed the seventh day, and
__ __ __ __ __ __ __ __ __ __ it: because that in it he had
rested from all his work which God created and made.

```
S N I Q S E U E L T T A C E P
C R S E H S I N E L P E R E D
R I A L T S I H T X I S E C I
N A E N O N F T F L E E E N S
O F T O G E I F C V E H P L S
I L L I N V S E E D W T E I A
N D T S I A G N O A T F T A N
I E B L N E T G E E N O H A C
M T U L E H F R U I T F U L T
O S Q Y V O O E V E S T W E I
D E T A E R C O G U L H S I F
I R S G A N O P R A D E I G I
H E A R T H D A L T M A A B E
V M I E S T S N R N E I D T D
I A N C L C A L T I U R F H S
```

5. ADAM

Genesis 2:7-17

And the LORD God __ __ __ __ __ __ man of the dust of the ground, and breathed into his __ __ __ __ __ __ __ __ the breath of life; and man became a __ __ __ __ __ __ __ __ __ __ (2w). **8** And the LORD God planted a garden eastward in __ __ __ __; and there he put the man whom he had formed. **9** And out of the ground made the LORD God to grow every tree that is pleasant to the sight, and good for food; the __ __ __ __ __ __ __ __ __ __ (3w) also in the midst of the garden, and the tree of __ __ __ __ __ __ __ __ __ of good and evil. **10** And a __ __ __ __ __ went out of Eden to water the garden; and from thence it was parted, and became into __ __ __ __ __ __ __ __ __ (2w). **11** The name of the first is __ __ __ __ __: that is it which compasseth the whole land of __ __ __ __ __ __ __, where there is gold; **12** and the gold of that land is good: there is bdellium and the onyx stone. **13** And the name of the second river is __ __ __ __ __: the same is it that compasseth the whole land of Ethiopia. **14** And the name of the third river is

__ __ __ __ __ __ __ __: that is it which goeth toward the east of Assyria. And the fourth river is

__ __ __ __ __ __ __ __ __. **15** And the LORD God took the man, and put him into the __ __ __ __ __ __ of Eden to dress it and to keep it. **16** And the LORD God

__ __ __ __ __ __ __ __ __ the man, saying, Of every tree of the garden thou mayest freely __ __ __: **17** but of the tree of the knowledge of __ __ __ __ and __ __ __ __, thou shalt not eat of it: for in the day that thou eatest thereof thou shalt surely

__ __ __.

```
L E K E D D I H A V I L A H E
I T U Q S T I E I T E R E E U
V B K R A D O O G H A I E P P
I I N O S I P A Z E T A D F H
N M O R E T R N F O R M E D R
G B W G F D A I K B T A N E A
S E L O E Y L Y C W F I N D T
O D E N G F E G I H O N L N E
U S D W O W I C E E U C C A S
L E G E D S H T H L R I A M T
P R E I V E T T O E H E M M S
O R S A E F H R I V E R E O S
T D F B A D B L I I A H L C A
A R T Y N T F L N L D K E I L
D O E E W A Y N T O S I N H E
```

6. EVE

Genesis 2:18-25

And the LORD God said, It is not good that the man should
__ __ __ __ __ __ __ (2w); I will make him an help meet
for him. **19** And out of the ground the __ __ __ __ God formed
every beast of the __ __ __ __ __, and every __ __ __ __
of the air; and brought them unto __ __ __ __ to see what
he would call them: and whatsoever Adam called every living
__ __ __ __ __ __ __ __, that was the name thereof.
20 And Adam gave names to all __ __ __ __ __ __, and to
the fowl of the air, and to every beast of the field; but for Adam
there was not found an __ __ __ __   __ __ __ __ (2w)
for him. **21** And the LORD God caused a deep __ __ __ __ __
to fall upon Adam, and he slept: and he took __ __ __   __ __
__ __ __   __ __ __ __ (4w), and closed up the flesh
instead thereof; **22** and the rib, which the LORD God had taken
from man, made he a woman, and __ __ __ __ __ __ __
her unto the man. **23** And Adam said, This is now bone of my
__ __ __ __ __, and flesh of my __ __ __ __ __: she shall
be called __ __ __ __ __, because she was taken out of Man.
24 Therefore shall a man leave his __ __ __ __ __ __ and his
__ __ __ __ __ __, and shall cleave unto his __ __ __ __: and
they shall be __ __ __   __ __ __ __ __ (2w). **25** And they
were both __ __ __ __ __, the man and his wife, and were not
__ __ __ __ __ __ __.

```
D H S E L F E N O O W I P R T
G O Q U D A S D N M L R E B H
O P T E E M P L E H T O C H M
A L L Y K E D E O T S N P A O
P E W O A N N O F N N E G M T
A Y O D N O G L H I E X L H H
S M F G L E U R I L H S G F E
H R I A N Y A W S H U U R U R
A I E R U T A E R C O A E S N
M B L W M F H A I R T G B N I
E F D O U N A Y B O N E S L E
D O N M R A R T S H T I F P P
A S G A O D A E H W L T C I R
L R C N C A T T L E Y P K A W
Z O P T N M R A I F R H L L E
```

7. THE TEMPTATION OF EVE

Genesis 3:1-8

Now the serpent was more subtil than any __ __ __ __ __
of the field which the LORD God had made. And he said unto
the __ __ __ __ __, Yea, hath God said, Ye shall not
eat of every tree of the __ __ __ __ __ __? **2** And the
woman said unto the __ __ __ __ __ __ __, We may
eat of the __ __ __ __ __ __ __ __ __ __
__ __ __ __ __ (4w) of the garden: **3** But of the fruit of the
tree which is in the midst of the garden, God hath said, __ __
__ __ __ __ __ __ __ __ __ __ __ (4w) of it,
neither shall ye __ __ __ __ __ it, lest ye die. **4** And the
serpent said unto the woman, Ye shall not __ __ __ __ __ __
__ __ __ (2w): **5** for God doth know that in the day ye eat thereof,
then your eyes shall be __ __ __ __ __ __, and ye shall be
as gods, knowing __ __ __ __ and __ __ __ __. **6** And
when the woman saw that the tree was good for food, and that it
was __ __ __ __ __ __ __ __ to the eyes, and a tree to be
desired to make one __ __ __ __, she took of the fruit thereof,
and did eat, and gave also unto her __ __ __ __ __ __ __
with her; and he did eat. **7** And the __ __ __ __ of them both
were opened, and they knew that they were __ __ __ __ __;
and they sewed __ __ __ __ __ __ __ __ __ (2w)
together, and made themselves aprons. **8** And they heard the voice
of the LORD God walking in the garden in the __ __ __ __
__ __ __ __ __ __ __ __ (4w): and Adam and his wife
hid themselves from the __ __ __ __ __ __ __ __ of the
__ __ __ __ __ __ __ (2w) amongst the trees of the garden.

```
N T Y A D E H T F O L O O C A
G R O I Q U L O R D G O D S D
N B T S E R P E N T U L B E M
P K B H B B E O S A R W N V R
L A I E N G N C I E D E K A N
E L E D A S R P R T P K E E P
A T P R W S U T G O M A S L R
S Y D T O P T R C N D O O G E
A E R N M C L A E L L X S I S
N Y V C A R W W T L R T M F E
T E H I N B I Y O A Y K T C N
B S A H L E S B U H L D K N C
A N I W U Q E U C S L I I N E
F R U I T O F T H E T R E E S
B O S E M N O Z A Y G O N A N
```

8. NOAH AND THE ARK

Genesis 6:13-22

And God said unto ___ ___ ___ ___, The end of all

flesh is come before me; for the earth is filled with

___ ___ ___ ___ ___ ___ ___ ___ through them; and, behold, I will

___ ___ ___ ___ ___ ___ ___ them with the earth. **14** Make thee

an ark of ___ ___ ___ ___ ___ ___ ___ ___ ___ ___ (2w); rooms

shalt thou make in the ark, and shalt pitch it within and without with

pitch. **15** And this is the fashion which thou shalt make it of: The

___ ___ ___ ___ ___ ___ of the ark shall be three hundred cubits, the

___ ___ ___ ___ ___ ___ ___ of it fifty ___ ___ ___ ___ ___ ___,

and the ___ ___ ___ ___ ___ ___ of it thirty cubits. **16** A window

shalt thou make to the ark, and in a cubit shalt thou finish it above; and

the door of the ark shalt thou set in the side thereof; with lower, second,

and ___ ___ ___ ___ ___ stories shalt thou make it. **17** And, behold,

I, even I, do bring a ___ ___ ___ ___ ___ of waters upon the earth, to

destroy all flesh, wherein is the ___ ___ ___ ___ ___ ___ ___ ___

___ ___ ___ ___ (3w), from under heaven; and every thing that is in

the earth ___ ___ ___ ___ ___ ___ ___ ___ (2w). **18** But with thee

will I establish my ___ ___ ___ ___ ___ ___ ___ ___; and thou shalt

come into the ___ ___ ___ , thou, and thy sons, and thy wife, and

thy sons' wives with thee. **19** And of every ___ ___ ___ ___ ___ ___

___ ___ ___ ___ ___ (2w) of all flesh, ___ ___ ___ ___ ___

___ ___ ___ ___ ___ ___ ___ ___ ___ (4w) shalt thou bring

into the ark, to keep them alive with thee; they shall be male and

___ ___ ___ ___ ___ ___. **20** Of fowls after their kind, and of

cattle after their kind, of every creeping thing of the earth after his

kind, two of every sort shall come unto thee, to ___ ___ ___ ___

___ ___ ___ ___ ___ ___ (3w). **21** And take thou unto

```
T N A N E V O C E D Y M G P M
W I L E I D L L A H S C K E D
O E I A W L K B R E A D T H A
O V V D S B I T J N O D D T R
F I I E A R U K B O U H A G V
E L N D B E R T W A R E C N I
V A G N L A S R H H T I H E N
E M T A I T E T T N J G T L W
R E H M D H H W O I C H X W R
Y H I M P O P C U B I T S D O
S T N O N F H E M R K E A G I
O P G C F L O O D E S T R O Y
R E W L U I T Z P U N L E A S
T E D S Q F E M A L E B C E O
A K A H L E C N E L O I V M C
```

thee of all food that is eaten, and thou shalt gather it to thee; and it shall be for food for thee, and for them. **22** Thus did Noah; according to all that God __ __ __ __ __ __ __ __ __ him, so did he.

9. THE PROMISE

Genesis 8:1, 15-22

And God remembered __ __ __ __, and every living thing,
and all the cattle that was with him in the ark. . . . **15** And God
__ __ __ __ __ unto Noah, saying, **16** Go forth of the ark,
thou, and thy wife, and thy sons, and thy sons' wives with thee.
17 Bring forth with thee every living thing that is with thee,
of all flesh, both of fowl, and of cattle, and of every creeping
thing that __ __ __ __ __ __ __ __ upon the earth;
that they may __ __ __ __ __ abundantly in the earth,
and be fruitful, and __ __ __ __ __ __ __ __ upon
the __ __ __ __ __. **18** And Noah went forth, and his
__ __ __ __, and his __ __ __ __, and his sons' wives
with him: **19** every beast, every creeping thing, and every fowl, and
whatsoever creepeth upon the earth, after their kinds, went forth
__ __ __ __ __ __ __ __ __ (4w).
20 And Noah builded an __ __ __ __ __ unto the LORD;
and took of every clean beast, and of every clean fowl, and offered
__ __ __ __ __ __ __ __ __ __ __ __ __ (2w)
on the altar. **21** And the LORD smelled a __ __ __ __ __
__ __ __ __ __ __ (2w); and the LORD said in his heart,
I will not again __ __ __ __ __ the ground any more for
man's sake; for the __ __ __ __ __ __ __ __ __ __ __
of man's heart is evil from his __ __ __ __ __; neither
will I again __ __ __ __ __ any more every thing living,
as I have done. **22** While the earth remaineth, seedtime and
__ __ __ __ __ __ __, and cold and __ __ __ __,
and summer and __ __ __ __ __ __, and day and
__ __ __ __ __ shall not cease.

```
L O O E S R U C R O U L S T U
O D G S N O A H O W A L T A R
V M H D O I T O K F I R K B E
M A N T S E V R A H N I W K T
U C R H R Q U J Y D E R R S N
L E A G A A K G N I A A S E I
T K T I Z P E K D S E G T V W
I A S N Y P W O T H C D E I B
P P R U O V A S T E E W S N G
L S G N I R E F F O T N R U B
Y M P H H A O O R B O L W W R
O I N O I T A N I G A M I D E
R T H T U O Y E E C H R F C E
R E S O H T E P E E R C E N D
B X S N I R P T Z O M Y S X O
```

10. GOD'S COVENANT WITH ABRAM

Genesis 12:1-3; 15:18-21

Now the Lord had said unto __ __ __ __ __, Get thee out of
thy __ __ __ __ __ __ __, and from thy kindred, and from
thy father's __ __ __ __ __, unto a land that I will shew thee:
2 and I will make of thee a great __ __ __ __ __ __, and I will
__ __ __ __ __ thee, and make thy name __ __ __ __ __;
and thou shalt be a blessing: **3** and I will bless them that bless thee,
and __ __ __ __ __ him that __ __ __ __ __ __ __
thee: and in thee shall all __ __ __ __ __ __ __ __ of the
earth be blessed. . . . **18** In the same day the __ __ __ __ made
a __ __ __ __ __ __ __ __ with Abram, saying, Unto thy
seed have I given this __ __ __ __, from the river of Egypt unto
the great river, the river __ __ __ __ __ __ __ __ __:
19 the __ __ __ __ __ __ __, and the
__ __ __ __ __ __ __ __ __ __, and the
Kadmonites, **20** and the __ __ __ __ __ __ __ __,
and the __ __ __ __ __ __ __ __ __ __,
and the __ __ __ __ __ __ __ __, **21** and the
__ __ __ __ __ __ __ __, and the Canaanites, and the
Girgashites, and the __ __ __ __ __ __ __ __ __.

```
H E O M N L F A M I L I E S M
S L M A C L O I S E T I N E K
R L D R I B R M E X E K T T Z
E E T B S H B W T P S S T I Z
P C H A S L K E A L Y A R S E
H Z I O E D N S R O A E T U S
A Z V S T R D O H R G N R B C
I T S D I B G Z P D A I D E O
M D E P Z G E Z U N M U S J U
S E T I Z Z I N E K O B E N N
R H I S I A H V D J R I S E T
O I T T R L O C H E I F U S R
H G T C E C G O N A T I O N Y
C R I K P Z D M A S E T H S L
M W H T E S R U C B S T G H S
```

11. ABRAHAM AND ISAAC

Genesis 22:1-2, 6-13

And it __ __ __ __   __ __   __ __ __ __ (3w)
after these things, that God did tempt Abraham, and said unto
him, Abraham: and he said, Behold, here I am. **2** And he said,
Take now thy son, thine only son __ __ __ __ __, whom
thou __ __ __ __ __ __, and get thee into the land of
__ __ __ __ __ __; and offer him there for a burnt offering
upon one of the __ __ __ __ __ __ __ __ __ __ which I will
tell thee of. . . . **6** And __ __ __ __ __ __ __ took the wood of
the __ __ __ __ __   __ __ __ __ __ __ __ __ (2w),
and laid it upon Isaac his son; and he took the fire in his hand, and a
knife; and they went both of them together. **7** And Isaac spake unto
Abraham his father, and said, __ __   __ __ __ __ __ __:
and he said, Here am I, my son. And he said, Behold the fire
and the __ __ __ __: but where is the __ __ __ __
for a burnt offering? **8** And Abraham said, My son, God will
__ __ __ __ __ __ __ himself a lamb for a burnt offering:
so they went both of them __ __ __ __ __ __ __ __.
9 And they came to the place which God had told him of; and
Abraham built an __ __ __ __ __ there, and laid the wood
in order, and bound Isaac his son, and laid him on the altar upon
the wood. **10** And Abraham stretched forth his hand, and took the
__ __ __ __ __ to slay his son. **11** And the __ __ __ __ __
__ __   __ __ __   __ __ __ __ (4w) called unto him
out of __ __ __ __ __ __, and said, Abraham, Abraham: and
he said, Here am I. **12** And he said, Lay not thine hand upon the
lad, neither do thou any thing unto him: for now I know that thou
__ __ __ __ __ __ __ God, seeing thou hast not withheld

```
M O D K O L C O Q U S M S O R
A N G E L O F T H E L O R D A
H E C M I V W O O D Y R A S G
A V F O N E A G F H M I M D N
R A S E S S T E T A T A L L I
B E M N C T A T N E K H O O R
A H O V A R C H Y B K P J U E
I S U L E E O E S A M C A D F
R V N S E H S R R L C T I N F
E F T Q N T K A E T E V S H O
A S A U C A N B M A O P A K T
R T I A T F I W S R S T A C N
S E N P P Y F K P C R A C N R
X T S C A M E T O P A S S C U
N I C D N O A P H I N L A M B
```

thy son, thine only son from me. **13** And Abraham lifted up his
___ ___ ___ ___, and looked, and behold behind him a ram caught in
a ___ ___ ___ ___ ___ ___ ___ by his horns: and Abraham went and
took the ___ ___ ___, and offered him up for a burnt offering in the
stead of his son.

12. JACOB AND ESAU

Genesis 25:21-34

And Isaac intreated the LORD for his wife, because
she was __ __ __ __ __ __: and the LORD was
__ __ __ __ __ __ __ __ __ of him, and Rebekah his wife
conceived. **22** And the children __ __ __ __ __ __ __ __ __
together within her; and she said, If it be so, why am I thus?
And she went to enquire of the LORD. **23** And the LORD said
unto her, __ __ __ __ __ __ __ __ __ __ (2w)
are in thy womb, and two manner of people shall be separated
from thy __ __ __ __ __ __; and the one people shall
be stronger than the other people; and the elder shall serve the
__ __ __ __ __ __ __. **24** And when her days to be
delivered were fulfilled, behold, there were __ __ __ __ __
in her womb. **25** And the first came out red, all over like an
__ __ __ __ __   __ __ __ __ __ __ __ (2w); and
they called his name __ __ __ __. **26** And after that came his
brother out, and his hand took hold on Esau's __ __ __ __;
and his name was called __ __ __ __ __: and Isaac was
__ __ __ __ __ __ __ __ __ __ years old when
she bare them. **27** And the boys grew: and Esau was a cunning
__ __ __ __ __ __, a man of the field; and Jacob was a
plain man, dwelling in __ __ __ __ __. **28** And Isaac loved
Esau, because he did eat of his __ __ __ __ __ __ __:
but __ __ __ __ __ __ __ loved Jacob. **29** And Jacob sod
pottage: and Esau came from the field, and he was faint: **30** And
Esau said to Jacob, __ __ __ __   __ __ (2w), I pray thee,
with that same red pottage; for I am __ __ __ __ __: therefore
was his name called Edom. **31** And Jacob said, Sell me this day thy

S W O B S N O I T A N O W T C
E D T O E I N T R E A T E D H
S R I W C I S P R O K O R A T
E C F E E D M E X E O B H L H
L D O L D M G R N L L A T A E
I E R S I N Y O A B K R I E E
T S P L U D S C I E B R D J L
N P A O F I O S B U Y E N H B
E I Y H N L S E S G O N T T N
L S E E C P R E A T F D D Z H
J E V F S P O R P H N I U C I
A D T A A A M H U N T E R K L
C N E I I E U T S N I W T M S
O B R N N H S T R U G G L E D
B I R T H R I G H T P H C A T

___ ___ ___ ___ ___ ___ ___ ___ ___ ___. **32** and Esau said, Behold, I am at the point to die: and what ___ ___ ___ ___ ___ ___ shall this birthright do to me? **33** And Jacob said, Swear to me this day; and he sware unto him: and he sold his birthright unto Jacob. **34** Then Jacob gave Esau bread and pottage of ___ ___ ___ ___ ___ ___ ___ ___; and he did eat and drink, and rose up, and went his way: thus Esau ___ ___ ___ ___ ___ ___ ___ ___ his birthright.

13. MOSES IN THE BASKET

Exodus 2:1-10

And there went a man of the __ __ __ __ __   __ __
__ __ __ __ (3w), and took to wife a daughter of Levi. **2** And the
woman conceived, and __ __ __ __   __   __ __ __ (3w):
and when she saw him that he was a __ __ __ __ __ __ child,
she hid him __ __ __ __ __   __ __ __ __ __ __ (2w).
3 And when she could not longer hide him, she took for him
an ark of __ __ __ __ __ __ __ __ __, and daubed
it with slime and with __ __ __ __ __, and put the child
therein; and she laid it in the flags by the river's brink. **4** And his
__ __ __ __ __ __ stood afar off, to wit what would be done
to him. **5** And the daughter of __ __ __ __ __ __ __ came
down to __ __ __ __   __ __ __ __ __ __ __ (2w)
at the river; and her maidens walked along by the river's
side; and when she saw the ark among the flags, she sent her
__ __ __ __ to fetch it. **6** And when she had opened it, she saw
the __ __ __ __ __: and, behold, the babe wept. And she had
__ __ __ __ __ __ __ __ __ __ on him, and said, This is
one of the Hebrews' __ __ __ __ __ __ __ __. **7** Then said his
sister to Pharaoh's __ __ __ __ __ __ __ __, Shall I go and
call to thee a nurse of the __ __ __ __ __ __ women, that she
may nurse the child for thee? **8** And Pharaoh's daughter said to her,
Go. And the maid went and called the child's mother. **9** And Pharaoh's
daughter said unto her, Take this child away, and nurse it for me, and
I will give thee __ __ __   __ __ __ __ __ (2w). And the
women took the child, and __ __ __ __ __ __   __ __ (2w).
10 And the child __ __ __ __, and she brought him unto
Pharaoh's daughter, and he __ __ __ __ __ __ __   __ __

```
I  H  O  U  S  E  O  F  L  E  V  I  C  S  O
O  D  W  G  F  L  E  S  R  E  H  H  S  A  W
D  H  R  R  A  S  T  D  Y  H  P  A  C  O  R
G  T  I  E  T  N  M  L  W  E  C  O  H  S  P
M  I  H  W  E  R  D  I  T  S  M  Q  I  C  H
A  D  C  M  R  O  E  H  E  P  U  S  L  D  E
I  E  T  A  O  L  L  C  A  S  T  N  D  A  T
D  S  I  G  W  E  A  S  C  E  O  Y  R  U  G
C  R  P  A  E  R  S  J  R  S  A  T  E  G  W
E  U  H  Y  U  I  P  H  A  C  K  I  N  H  E
S  N  A  Q  O  L  S  E  G  A  W  Y  H  T  R
E  I  R  N  O  S  R  E  H  E  M  A  C  E  B
S  G  A  B  O  A  D  Z  F  F  Y  N  S  R  E
O  H  O  N  B  U  L  R  U  S  H  E  S  M  H
M  T  H  R  E  E  M  O  N  T  H  S  D  O  X
```

___ ___ ___ (3w). And she called his name ___ ___ ___ ___ ___: and she said, Because I ___ ___ ___ ___ ___ ___ ___ (2w) out of the water.

14. MOSES AND THE BURNING BUSH

Exodus 3:1-8

Now Moses kept the flock of Jethro his ___ ___ ___ ___ ___ ___
___ ___ ___ ___ ___ (3w), the priest of ___ ___ ___ ___ ___ ___:
and he led the ___ ___ ___ ___ ___ to the backside of the desert,
and came to the ___ ___ ___ ___ ___ ___ ___ ___ of God, even to
Horeb. **2** And the ___ ___ ___ ___ ___ ___ ___ ___ ___ ___
___ ___ ___ ___ (4w) appeared unto him in a flame of fire out
of the midst of a ___ ___ ___ ___: and he looked, and, behold,
the bush burned with ___ ___ ___ ___, and the bush was not
___ ___ ___ ___ ___ ___ ___ ___. **3** And ___ ___ ___ ___ ___
said, I will now turn aside, and see this great sight, why the bush is not
burnt. **4** And when the Lord saw that he turned aside to see, God
called unto him out of the midst of the bush, and said, Moses, Moses.
And he said, Here am I. **5** And he said, Draw not nigh hither: put
off thy ___ ___ ___ ___ ___ from off thy feet, for the place whereon
thou standest is ___ ___ ___ ___ ___ ___ ___ ___ ___ ___ (2w).
6 Moreover he said, I am the God of thy father, the God of
___ ___ ___ ___ ___ ___ ___, the God of ___ ___ ___ ___ ___, and
the God of ___ ___ ___ ___ ___. And Moses hid his ___ ___ ___ ___;
for he was afraid to look upon God. **7** And the Lord said, I have surely
seen the ___ ___ ___ ___ ___ ___ ___ ___ ___ ___ of my people which
are in ___ ___ ___ ___ ___, and have heard their cry by reason of their
taskmasters; for I know their ___ ___ ___ ___ ___ ___ ___; **8** and I am
come down to deliver them out of the hand of the Egyptians, and to bring
them up out of that land unto a good land and a large, unto a land flowing
with ___ ___ ___ ___ ___ ___ ___ ___ ___ ___ ___ ___ (3w);
unto the place of the ___ ___ ___ ___ ___ ___ ___ ___ ___ ___, and
the Hittites, and the Amorites, and the Perizzites, and the Hivites, and the
Jebusites.

```
S O R B O U B M O U N T A I N
P K A S D C U A L T L U R A O
T C E A T U S L M I D I A N I
A O F F A T H E R I N L A W T
C N O I L E E T S M U E O R C
A S S S H O E S P H O Y R K I
N U W T H E C S N Y R W O I L
A M O S E S C K E L G E C A F
A E R N A Q U H S L Y E E W F
N D R O L E H T F O L E G N A
I B O G G D A J B B O W X A B
T C S M I L K A N D H O N E Y
E O E L O X D C A A S I S T A
S R T G H C C O R B A U Z I Y
L L B W A K A B R A H A M A N
```

15. THE CROSSING OF THE RED SEA

Exodus 14:21-23, 26-31

And Moses stretched out his hand over the sea; and the
Lord caused the sea to go back by a strong ___ ___ ___ ___
___ ___ ___ ___ (2w) all that night, and made the sea
___ ___ ___ ___ ___ ___ ___ (2w), and the waters were
___ ___ ___ ___ ___ ___ ___. **22** And the children of Israel went
into the midst of the sea upon the dry ___ ___ ___ ___ ___ ___:
and the waters were a wall unto them on their right hand, and
on their ___ ___ ___ ___. **23** And the Egyptians pursued,
and went in after them to the midst of the sea, even all
Pharaoh's horses, his ___ ___ ___ ___ ___ ___ ___ ___,
and his ___ ___ ___ ___ ___ ___ ___ ___. . . . **26** And the
Lord said unto ___ ___ ___ ___ ___, Stretch out thine
hand over the sea, that the waters may come again upon the
___ ___ ___ ___ ___ ___ ___ ___ ___, upon their chariots,
and upon their horsemen. **27** And Moses stretched forth his
hand over the sea, and the sea returned to his strength when the
___ ___ ___ ___ ___ ___ ___ appeared; and the Egyptians fled
against it; and the Lord ___ ___ ___ ___ ___ ___ ___ ___ ___
the Egyptians in the midst of the sea. **28** And the waters returned,
and ___ ___ ___ ___ ___ ___ ___ the chariots, and the horsemen,
and all the host of ___ ___ ___ ___ ___ ___ ___ that came into
the sea after them; there remained not so much as one of them.
29 But the children of ___ ___ ___ ___ ___ ___ walked upon
dry land in the midst of the sea; and the waters were a wall unto
them on their ___ ___ ___ ___ ___ hand, and on their left.
30 Thus the Lord ___ ___ ___ ___ ___ Israel that day out of the
___ ___ ___ ___ of the Egyptians; and Israel saw the Egyptians

```
G Y B S I R L O G F A I N G D
G D E R E V O C D N A L Y R D
D O L A O R M I S R A E L O N
N O I P S A V E D O B E H U I
C M E Z Y I S L N Y F O E N W
H R V S D P S P A T A V B D T
A X E E N Q U A H R W E P I S
R S D A G E S G A T U R G D A
I E S S B Y I H R T H T C K E
O S T H X R P P H K C H Y M C
T O V O R Q U T F E A R E D K
S M O R N I N G I R E E N F A
R M N E A Q U H D A F W R B L
A G H R A I N A Z T N C H U T
B T G L L Z G N E M E S R O H
```

dead upon the __ __ __   __ __ __ __ __ (2w).

31 And Israel saw that great work which the LORD did upon the Egyptians: and the people __ __ __ __ __ __ the LORD, and __ __ __ __ __ __ __ __ the LORD, and his servant Moses.

16. SAMUEL'S CALLING

1 Samuel 3:2-11, 19-21

And it came to pass at that time, when Eli was laid down in his
place, and his eyes began to ___ ___ ___   ___ ___ ___ (2w), that
he could not see; **3** and ere the ___ ___ ___ ___ of God went out
in the ___ ___ ___ ___ ___ ___ of the LORD, where the ark of God
was, and Samuel was laid down to sleep; **4** that the LORD called
___ ___ ___ ___ ___ ___: and he answered, Here am I. **5** And he
ran unto Eli, and said, ___ ___ ___ ___   ___ ___   ___ (3w);
for thou calledst me. And he said, I called not; lie down again.
And he went and ___ ___ ___   ___ ___ ___ ___ (2w). **6** And the
LORD called yet again, Samuel. And Samuel ___ ___ ___ ___ ___
and went to Eli, and said, Here am I; for thou didst call me. And
he answered, I called not, my son; lie down again. **7** Now Samuel
did not yet know the LORD, neither was the word of the LORD yet
___ ___ ___ ___ ___ ___ ___ ___ unto him. **8** And the LORD called
Samuel again the ___ ___ ___ ___ ___ time. And he arose and
went to Eli, and said, Here am I; for thou didst call me. And Eli
___ ___ ___ ___ ___ ___ ___ ___ ___ that the LORD had called the
child. **9** Therefore Eli said unto Samuel, Go, lie down: and it shall be,
if he call thee, that thou shalt say, ___ ___ ___ ___ ___, LORD; for
thy ___ ___ ___ ___ ___ ___ ___ heareth. So Samuel went and lay
down in his place. **10** And the LORD came, and stood, and called as at
other times, Samuel, Samuel. Then Samuel answered, Speak; for thy
servant ___ ___ ___ ___ ___ ___ ___. **11** And the LORD said to Samuel,
Behold, I will do a thing in ___ ___ ___ ___ ___ ___, at which both
the ears of every one that heareth it shall ___ ___ ___ ___ ___ ___. . . .
19 And Samuel ___ ___ ___ ___, and the LORD was with him, and
did let none of his words fall to the ground. **20** And all Israel from

```
E D E I L N V E R E W D Z N G
C H R C U S S H I L O H H R S
D I K D E L A E V E R U S B O
E T M D A S T L M I D X A W N
V R L A Y D O W N T O N R A O
I S R A E L G O H O F S O N D
E S S P L R Y F U B T T S L L
C E B N E O E T Q Y H P E E X
R R S W A B E H S R E E B E T
E V A E N M U I L A L L R I U
P A M S P D D R K A O G L D A
P N U L T T O D M O R N D F L
Z T E H P O R P P I D I N E S
F I L A P T H E A R E T H O G
N G A M D A U L T H G T D N E
```

Dan even to __ __ __ __ __ __ __ __ __ knew that Samuel
was established to be a __ __ __ __ __ __ __ of the LORD.
21 And the LORD appeared again in __ __ __ __ __ __: for the
LORD revealed himself to Samuel in Shiloh by the __ __ __ __
__ __ __ __ __ __ __ __ (4w).

17. DAVID AND GOLIATH

1 Samuel 17:45-51

Then said David to the ___ ___ ___ ___ ___ ___ ___ ___ ___ ___,
Thou comest to me with a ___ ___ ___ ___ ___, and with a spear,
and with a shield: but I come to thee in the name of the LORD of
hosts, the God of the armies of ___ ___ ___ ___ ___ ___, whom
thou hast ___ ___ ___ ___ ___ ___. **46** This day will the LORD
___ ___ ___ ___ ___ ___ ___ thee into mine hand; and I will
___ ___ ___ ___ ___   ___ ___ ___ ___ (2w), and take thine head
from thee; and I will give the carcases of the host of the Philistines this
day unto the fowls of the air, and to the wild ___ ___ ___ ___ ___ ___
of the earth; that all the earth may know that there is a God in Israel.
47 And all this ___ ___ ___ ___ ___ ___ ___ ___ shall know that the
LORD saveth not with sword and ___ ___ ___ ___ ___: for the battle
is the LORD's, and he will give you ___ ___ ___ ___   ___ ___ ___
___ ___ ___ ___ ___ (3w). **48** And it came to pass, when the Philistine
arose, and came, and drew nigh to meet David, that David hastened,
and ran toward the ___ ___ ___ ___ to meet the Philistine. **49** And
David put his hand in his bag, and took thence a ___ ___ ___ ___ ___,
and slang it, and smote the Philistine in his forehead, that the stone
sunk into his ___ ___ ___ ___ ___ ___ ___; and he fell upon his
face to the earth. **50** So David ___ ___ ___ ___ ___ ___ ___ ___ ___
over the Philistine with a ___ ___ ___ ___ ___ and with a
stone, and smote the Philistine, and slew him; but there was
no sword in the hand of David. **51** Therefore David ran, and
___ ___ ___ ___ ___   ___ ___ ___ ___ (2w) the Philistine, and
took his sword, and drew it out of the ___ ___ ___ ___ ___ ___
thereof, and slew him, and ___ ___ ___   ___ ___ ___   ___ ___ ___

```
R E V I L E D E L I A V E R P
L E D A E H S I H F F O T U C
S H E A T H C F A V C E I T R
S A A O E S T O N E E N D A I
P W D K I D W A S H T Y E R A
Y C O H V N L O B A R P F M R
A H S T S A E B R I S H I Y R
E A A N T H C K T D H I E H E
D M L F O R E H E A D L D I S
R P O R H U G E L F Y I N N S
T I O X E O Y L B M E S S A K
N O P U D O O T S R D T L E O
F N S Z D T L E A R S I I F U
R H U C E N A Y C B T N N W D
M O Q S M I T E T H E E G N R
```

___ ___ ___ ___ (4w) therewith. And when the Philistines saw their

___ ___ ___ ___ ___ ___ ___ ___ was ___ ___ ___ ___, they fled.

18. DANIEL AND THE LIONS' DEN

Daniel 6:16–23, 28

Then the king __ __ __ __ __ __ __ __ __, and
they brought Daniel, and cast him into the __ __ __
__ __ __ __ __ __ __ (3w). Now the king spake and
said unto Daniel, Thy God whom thou servest continually, he
will __ __ __ __ __ __ __ __ __ __ __ (2w).
17 And a __ __ __ __ __ was brought, and laid upon
the mouth of the den; and the king sealed it with his own

__ __ __ __ __ __, and with the signet of his lords;
that the purpose might not be changed concerning Daniel.
18 Then the king went to his __ __ __ __ __ __, and
passed the night __ __ __ __ __ __ __: neither were
__ __ __ __ __ __ __ __ __ __ __ __ of musick brought
before him: and his sleep went from him. **19** Then the king arose
very early in the __ __ __ __ __ __ __, and went in haste
unto the den of lions. **20** And when he came to the den, he cried
with a __ __ __ __ __ __ __ __ __ __ voice unto
Daniel: and the king spake and said to __ __ __ __ __ __,
O Daniel, servant of the living God, is thy God, whom thou
servest __ __ __ __ __ __ __ __ __ __ __, able to
deliver thee from the lions? **21** Then said Daniel unto the king, O
king, __ __ __ __ __ __ __ __ __ __ __ (3w).
22 My God hath sent his __ __ __ __ __, and hath shut
the lions' __ __ __ __ __ __, that they have not hurt
me: forasmuch as before him innocency was found in me;
and also before thee, O king, have I done no hurt. **23** Then
was the king __ __ __ __ __ __ __ __ __ __ __
__ __ __ __ (2w) for him, and commanded that they should take

```
I A P S F E N R G N I T S A F
E R A I N S T R U M E N T S R
D A L G Y L G N I D E E C X E
E T A N G E L O E E K B O K V
N B C E J O G D E L U Q N I E
O C E T E P N A L I G L T V R
F R A C R A I R B V U N I H O
L A U I M H N I A E P W N A F
I T H M T R R U T R E Z U D E
O E O S S T O S N T R Z A J V
N C D T T H M A E H S N L L I
S H T U O M W R M E I E L P L
S Y S I N I T X A E A A Y U C
G O S R E P R O L F N B D E T
M D O C R D E R E P S O R P N
```

Daniel up out of the den. So Daniel was taken up out of the den, and no manner of hurt was found upon him, because he believed in his God. . . . **28** So this Daniel __ __ __ __ __ __ __ __ __ in the reign of __ __ __ __ __ __, and in the reign of Cyrus the __ __ __ __ __ __ __.

19. TOWER OF BABEL

Genesis 11:1-9

And the whole earth was of one __ __ __ __ __ __ __ __ __,
and of one speech. **2** And it __ __ __ __ __ __
__ __ __ __ (3w), as they journeyed from the east, that they found
a plain in the land of __ __ __ __ __ __; and they dwelt there.
3 And they said one to __ __ __ __ __ __ __, Go to, let us
make __ __ __ __ __, and burn them thoroughly. And they had
brick for stone, and slime had they for morter. **4** And they said, Go
to, let us __ __ __ __ __ us a city and a __ __ __ __ __,
whose top may reach unto __ __ __ __ __ __; and let
us make us a name, lest we be scattered abroad upon the face
of the whole __ __ __ __ __. **5** And the LORD came
down to see the __ __ __ __ and the tower, which the
__ __ __ __ __ __ __ __ __ __ __ __ __ (3w)
builded. **6** And the LORD said, Behold, the __ __ __ __ __ __
is one, and they have all one language; and this they begin to do:
and now nothing will be restrained from them, which they have
__ __ __ __ __ __ __ __ to do. **7** Go to, let us go down,
and there __ __ __ __ __ __ __ __ their language,
that they may not __ __ __ __ __ __ __ __ __ __
one another's __ __ __ __ __ __. **8** So the LORD
__ __ __ __ __ __ __ __ __ them abroad from thence upon
the __ __ __ __ of all the earth: and they left off to build the
city. **9** Therefore is the name of it called __ __ __ __ __; because
the LORD did there confound the language of all the earth: and from
thence did the LORD scatter them __ __ __ __ __ __ upon the
face of all the earth.

```
C I F S S A P O T E M A C Y H
S Y E H B J I C K T W E H T U
K U N I A U E C T X I L I T N
E F E N L P I R P E O P L E D
W A G A S R B L E D L E D N E
K C I R B K F A D A E R R E R
L E I O P A D Y N N B S E H S
P H V T T E N G E O A R N T T
A L N N Y N U W H T B E O R A
C K A R P A O R S H S W F A N
H I S H G L F I R E E A M E D
D D N E M U N L E R S N E I T
I S E I K Q O H E A V E N T I
H C E E P S C A T T E R E D S
N T D E N I G A M I M E I M F
```

20. JACOB'S LADDER

Genesis 28:10-13, 15-16, 18-22

And Jacob went out from __ __ __ __ __ __ __ __ __,
and went toward Haran. **11** And he lighted upon a certain place, and
tarried there all night, because the sun was set; and he took of the
stones of that place, and put them for his pillows, and lay down in that
place to sleep. **12** And he __ __ __ __ __ __ __, and behold a
__ __ __ __ __ __ set up on the earth, and the top of it reached
to __ __ __ __ __ __: and behold the __ __ __ __ __ __
of God ascending and __ __ __ __ __ __ __ __ __ __
on it. **13** And, behold, the LORD stood above it, and said, I am the
LORD God of __ __ __ __ __ __ __ thy father, and the
God of __ __ __ __ __: the land whereon thou liest, to thee
will I give it, and to thy seed. . . . **15** And, behold, __ __ __
__ __ __ __ __ __ __ __ (4w), and will keep thee in
all places whither thou goest, and will bring thee again into this
land; for I will not leave thee, until I have done that which I have
spoken to thee of. **16** And __ __ __ __ __ awaked out of
his __ __ __ __ __, and he said, Surely the LORD is __ __
__ __ __ __ __ __ __ __ (3w); and I knew it not. . . .
18 And Jacob rose up early in the morning, and took the stone that he
had put for his __ __ __ __ __ __ __, and set it up for a pillar,
and poured oil upon the top of it. **19** And he called the name of that
place __ __ __ __ __ __: but the name of that city was called
Luz at the first. **20** And Jacob __ __ __ __ __ a vow, saying,
If God will be with me, and will keep me in this way that I go, and
will give me __ __ __ __ __ __ __ __ __ __ (3w),
and raiment to put on, **21** so that I come again to my father's house
in __ __ __ __ __; then shall the LORD __ __ __ __

```
G N I D N E C S E D E W O V N
A K N P E R T E N T H E U Q R
C T T A E O T D A E R B B T T
W A H C B A E I H E A V E N N
P E I R G R W T D S F R E Y Z
H R S P S B A D E M A E R D E
C A P T O R A H C N H A S O Y
N Y L C D L A I A T E Q H G S
E E A S T G E L H M C U E Y E
R J C L H A P T L R A I B M N
S L E E P H I N F I E E A E A
D B Z G S W O L L I P A C B S
E E C N M R I C A A S I O P U
G E K A X T E E A S S R Y W M
L L I E G E R N B E T H E L B
```

___ ___ ___ (3w): **22** And this stone, which I have set for a

___ ___ ___ ___ ___ ___, shall be God's house: and of all that thou

shalt give me I will surely give the ___ ___ ___ ___ ___ unto thee.

21. DAVID CHOSEN BY GOD

1 Samuel 16:1, 6–13

And the LORD said unto Samuel, How long wilt thou mourn for Saul, seeing I have rejected him from __ __ __ __ __ __ __ __ over Israel? fill thine __ __ __ __ __ __ __ __ __ __ __ (3w), and go, I will send thee to Jesse the __ __ __ __ __ __ __ __ __ __ __ __ __: for I have provided me a king among his sons. . . . **6** And it came to pass, when they were come, that he looked on Eliab, and said, Surely the LORD's __ __ __ __ __ __ __ __ is before him. **7** But the LORD said unto __ __ __ __ __ __, Look not on his countenance, or on the __ __ __ __ __ __ of his stature; because I have __ __ __ __ __ __ __ him: for the LORD seeth not as man seeth; for man looketh on the __ __ __ __ __ __ __ appearance, but the LORD looketh on the __ __ __ __ __. **8** Then Jesse called Abinadab, and made him pass before Samuel. And he said, Neither hath the __ __ __ __ chosen this. **9** Then __ __ __ __ __ made Shammah to pass by. And he said, Neither hath the LORD __ __ __ __ __ __ __ __ __ __ (2w). **10** Again, Jesse made seven __ __ __ __ __ __ __ __ __ (3w) to pass before Samuel. And Samuel said unto Jesse, The Lord hath not chosen these. **11** And Samuel said unto Jesse, Are here all thy __ __ __ __ __ __ __ __? And he said, There remaineth yet the __ __ __ __ __ __ __ __, and, behold, he keepeth the sheep. And Samuel said unto Jesse, Send and __ __ __ __ __ __ __ __ (2w): for we will not sit down till he come hither. **12** And he sent, and brought him in. Now he was ruddy, and withal of a beautiful __ __ __ __ __ __ __ __ __ __ __, and goodly

```
D A V I D R A W T U O S T R O
R E I G N I N G A D I R C K M
O T H T Z Q X B T I O H S E I
L H E I U U Q E A R N Y G P H
E V A O S I H T N E S O H C H
H O R N W I T H O I L U E O C
T F T D Y W E L I N R N I U T
F C H I L D R E N T E G G N E
O E L Y U E O H T L F E H T F
T D K T Q S U E E J U S T E S
I W H P E W D M D E S T O N V
R H C I N R P I A S E P W A E
I I A N O I N T Y S D H E N M
P R E L S F O E E E H G I C F
S N O S S I H F O H C T C E O
```

to look to. And the Lord said, Arise, ___ ___ ___ ___ ___ ___ him: for this is he. **13** Then Samuel took the horn of oil, and anointed him in the midst of his brethren: and the ___ ___ ___ ___ ___ ___ ___ ___ ___ ___ ___ ___ ___ ___ ___ (4w) came upon ___ ___ ___ ___ ___ from that day forward.

22. BATTLE OF JERICHO

Joshua 6:12-16, 20-21

And Joshua rose early in the __ __ __ __ __ __ __,
and the priests took up the ark of the LORD. **13** And seven
__ __ __ __ __ __ __ bearing __ __ __ __ __
__ __ __ __ __ __ __ __ __ (2w) of rams' horns before the
__ __ __ __ __ __ __ __ __ __ __ __ (4w)
went on continually, and __ __ __ __ with the trumpets: and the
armed men went before them; but the rereward came after the ark
of the LORD, the priests going on, and __ __ __ __ __ __ __
with the trumpets. **14** And the second day they compassed
the city once, and returned into the camp: so they did
__ __ __ __ __ __ __ (2w). **15** And it came to pass on the
__ __ __ __ __ __ __ day, that they __ __ __ __ early
about the __ __ __ __ __ __ __ __ __ __ __ __
__ __ __ (4w), and __ __ __ __ __ __ __ __ __ __
the city after the same manner seven times: only on that day
they compassed the city seven times. **16** And it came to pass
at the seventh time, when the priests blew with the trumpets,
__ __ __ __ __ __ said unto the people, __ __ __ __ __;
for the LORD hath given you the city. . . . **20** So the people
__ __ __ __ __ __ __ when the priests blew with the
trumpets: and it __ __ __ __ __ __ __ __ __ __ (3w),
when the people heard the sound of the trumpet, and the people
shouted with a __ __ __ __ __ __ __ __ __ __
(2w), that the wall __ __ __ __ __ __ __ __
__ __ __ __ (3w), so that the __ __ __ __ __ __ __
went up into the city, every man straight before him, and

```
A K N N S D E Y O R T S E D A
T U O H S T A E R G A H S A S
P R I E S T S O P U P O W W T
M Y O F A C S H H I L U H N E
K M H W E E R S S G N T C I P
S E C C Z L O I E B L E W N M
S H O U T J L X A V I D G G U
A M M O Q U G D T Q E N K O R
P L P Y G U H A O U I N C F T
O L A R N T P Y I W H R T T N
T M S D I T R S O U N S E H E
E L S G N E A L Y L E F L E V
M K E H R R B N D L M O L D E
A F D R O L E H T F O K R A S
C F R E M Y P E O P L E C Y T
```

they took the city. **21** And they __ __ __ __ __ __ __
__ __ __ __ __ __ __ __ __ all that was in the city.

23. SHADRACH, MESHACH, AND ABEDNEGO

Daniel 3:14-21, 24-25

Nebuchadnezzar spake and said unto them, Is it true, O Shadrach, Meshach, and Abednego, do not ye serve my gods, nor worship the __ __ __ __ __ __ __ __ __ __ __ (2w) which I have set up? **15** Now if ye be ready that at what time ye hear the sound of the cornet, __ __ __ __ __, harp, sackbut, psaltery, and __ __ __ __ __ __ __ __, and all kinds of musick, ye fall down and __ __ __ __ __ __ __ the image which I have made; well: but if ye worship not, ye shall be cast the same hour into the midst of a burning __ __ __ __ __ __ __ __ __ __ __ __ (2w); and who is that God that shall __ __ __ __ __ __ __ you out of my hands? **16** __ __ __ __ __ __ __ __ __, __ __ __ __ __ __ __ __, and __ __ __ __ __ __ __ __, answered and said to the king, O __ __ __ __ __ __ __ __ __ __ __ __ __ __ __, we are not careful to answer thee in this matter. **17** If it be so, our God whom we __ __ __ __ __ is able to deliver us from the burning fiery furnace, and he will deliver us out of thine hand, O king. **18** But if not, be it known unto thee, __ __ __ __ __ (2w), that we will not serve thy gods, nor worship the golden image which thou hast set up. **19** Then was Nebuchadnezzar full of __ __ __ __, and the form of his visage was changed against Shadrach, Meshach, and Abednego: therefore he spake, and commanded that they should heat the furnace one __ __ __ __ __ times more than it was wont to be heated. **20** And he __ __ __ __ __ __ __ __ __ the most __ __ __ __ __ __ men that were in his army to bind Shadrach, Meshach, and Abednego, and to cast them

```
B E C A N R U F Y R E I F S H
G O L D E N I M A G E E N A I
Y S P A N E M E E R H T W B E
I R A Z Z E N D A H C U B E N
W O R S H I P S E D T L I D L
T L V U Q F E H E B H F S N N
S L M E U R T D B V W E I E O
H E M G V H N U O M E P K G S
A S A E R A H L O K I N G O T
D N L L M I C C P H S X N J N
R U H M I N A I B D E O L E E
A O O C G O H M C A F S T M M
C C A Z H L S E K G N N C H R
H I F F T P E R O M S I L E A
O F U R Y V M D E L I V E R G
```

into the burning fiery furnace. **21** Then these men were bound
in their coats, their hosen, and their hats, and their other

__ __ __ __ __ __ __ __, and were cast into the midst of
the burning fiery furnace. . . . **24** Then Nebuchadnezzar the king
was astonished, and rose up in haste, and spake, and said unto his

__ __ __ __ __ __ __ __ __ __, Did not we cast

__ __ __ __ __ __ __ __ (2w) bound into the midst of
the fire? They answered and said unto the king, __ __ __ __, O
king. **25** He answered and said, Lo, I see four men loose, walking in the
midst of the fire, and they have no hurt; and the form of the fourth is
like the __ __ __ __ __ __ __ __ (3w).

24. JOSEPH'S COAT OF MANY COLORS

Genesis 37:3-5, 17-18, 23-24, 28, 31-34

Now __ __ __ __ __ __ loved Joseph more than all his
__ __ __ __ __ __ __ __, because he was the son of his
old age: and he made him a coat of many colours. **4** And when his
brethren saw that their __ __ __ __ __ __ loved him more
than all his brethren, they __ __ __ __ __ __ __ __ (2w),
and could not speak __ __ __ __ __ __ __ __ __ unto
him. **5** And Joseph __ __ __ __ __ __ __ a dream, and
he told it his brethren: and they hated him yet the more. . . .
17 And Joseph went after his __ __ __ __ __ __ __ __ __,
and found them in __ __ __ __ __ __. **18** And when
they saw him afar off, even before he came near unto them, they
__ __ __ __ __ __ __ __ __ __ against him to slay him. . . .
23 And it came to pass, when __ __ __ __ __ __ was come
unto his brethren, that they stript Joseph out of his __ __ __ __,
his coat of many colours that was on him; **24** and they took him, and
cast him __ __ __ __ __ __ __ __ (3w): and the pit
was empty, there was no __ __ __ __ __ in it. . . . **28** Then there
passed by Midianites __ __ __ __ __ __ __ __ __ __ __;
and they drew and lifted up Joseph out of the pit, and sold Joseph
to the Ishmeelites for twenty pieces of _ _ _ _ _ _: and they brought
Joseph into __ __ __ __ __. . . . **31** And they took Joseph's coat,
and killed a kid of the __ __ __ __ __, and dipped the coat in the
blood; **32** and they sent the coat of many colours, and they brought it
to their father; and said, This have we found: know now whether it be
thy son's coat or no. **33** And he knew it, and said, It is my son's coat;
an __ __ __ __ __ __ __ __ __ (2w) hath devoured him;
Joseph is without doubt rent in pieces. **34** And Jacob rent his clothes,

N	E	R	D	L	I	H	C	N	A	I	V	Y	O	H
A	H	A	T	E	D	H	I	M	Z	C	L	R	E	T
H	I	B	I	X	L	E	S	E	S	I	L	V	E	R
T	W	D	R	T	H	F	R	R	S	T	A	O	G	Z
O	P	R	E	R	P	E	A	C	E	A	B	L	Y	L
D	N	E	E	N	I	E	H	C	K	Q	U	P	I	I
E	Q	A	S	T	R	G	L	A	P	R	H	I	T	H
R	U	M	Z	H	X	U	B	N	C	E	U	N	I	R
I	A	E	R	S	L	A	O	T	L	T	S	T	K	Y
P	T	D	C	A	L	L	H	M	R	A	C	O	C	S
S	C	O	I	O	E	S	P	E	R	W	H	A	J	T
N	M	A	B	L	A	V	H	N	S	N	I	P	S	T
O	I	A	B	R	E	T	H	R	E	N	J	I	X	B
C	N	B	T	S	A	E	B	L	I	V	E	T	E	U
C	G	R	E	F	S	A	C	K	C	L	O	T	H	L

and put __ __ __ __ __ __ __ __ __ upon his loins, and __ __ __ __ __ __ __ for his son many days.

25. THE GOLDEN CALF

Exodus 32:7-8, 15-20

And the LORD said unto Moses, Go, get thee down; for thy
__ __ __ __ __ __, which thou broughtest out of the
land of __ __ __ __ __, have corrupted themselves:
8 they have turned aside quickly out of the way which I
__ __ __ __ __ __ __ __ __ them: they have made
them a molten __ __ __ __, and have worshipped it, and
have sacrificed thereunto, and said, These be thy gods, __
__ __ __ __ __ __ (2w), which have brought thee up out
of the land of Egypt. . . . **15** And __ __ __ __ __ turned, and
went down from the __ __ __ __ __, and the two tables of
the __ __ __ __ __ __ __ __ __ were in his hand: the
__ __ __ __ __ __ were written on both their sides; on the
one side and on the other were they __ __ __ __ __ __ __ _.
16 And the tables were the work of God, and the writing was
the writing of God, __ __ __ __ __ __ upon the tables.
17 And when Joshua heard the noise of the people as they shouted,
he said unto Moses, There is a __ __ __ __ __   __ __
__ __ __ (3w) in the camp. **18** And he said, It is not the voice
of them that shout for mastery, neither is it the voice of them that
cry for being __ __ __ __ __ __ __ __: but the noise
of them that sing do I hear. **19** And it came to pass, as soon as he
came nigh unto the __ __ __ __, that he saw the calf, and the
__ __ __ __ __ __ __: and Moses' anger __ __ __ __ __
hot, and he cast the tables out of his __ __ __ __ __, and
brake them beneath the mount. **20** And he took the calf which they
had made, and burnt it in the __ __ __ __, and ground it to
__ __ __ __ __ __, and strawed it upon the water, and made the
children of Israel __ __ __ __ __   __ __   __ __ (3w).

```
E G N I C N A D S P E E H I C
M A E D A G W A X E D T R L A
O S I P L R M O D R T N U O M
C D E D N A M M O C O T B E P
R T P O E V E A E I W O D N E
E G Y P T E N V S P S L S I E
V D C Q T N E E H C B R N T S
O R P U I A O R Y A E G A R Y
B I S O R F N I A L O B A E E
R N K A W O M B P F L Y R W L
A K T A L D S O K E B I R V A
L O R E Y I E S S R F T I O N
H F O G I P T R U E D O J H E
T I H Z Y N O M I T S E T C R
G T E H A N D S N E U A M K T
```

26. THE PROMISE OF ISAAC

Genesis 17: 1-9, 15-19

And when Abram was ninety years old and nine, the Lord
appeared to __ __ __ __ __, and said unto him, I am the
__ __ __ __ __ __ __ __   __ __ __ (2w); walk
before me, and be thou __ __ __ __ __ __ __. 2 And I
will make my __ __ __ __ __ __ __ __ between me and
thee, and will __ __ __ __ __ __ __ __ thee exceedingly.
3 And Abram fell on his face: and God talked with him, saying,
4 As for me, behold, my covenant is with thee, and thou shalt
be a father of many __ __ __ __ __ __ __. 5 Neither
shall thy name any more be called Abram, but thy name shall be
__ __ __ __ __ __ __; for a father of many nations have I
made thee. 6 And I will make thee exceeding fruitful, and I will make
nations of thee, and __ __ __ __ __ shall come out of thee.
7 And I will establish my covenant __ __ __ __ __ __ __
me and thee and thy seed after thee in their generations for an
__ __ __ __ __ __ __ __ __ __ covenant, to be
a God unto thee, and to thy seed after thee. 8 And I will give
unto thee, and to thy seed after thee, the land wherein thou art
a __ __ __ __ __ __ __ __, all the land of Canaan, for
an everlasting __ __ __ __ __ __ __ __ __ __; and
I will be their God. 9 And God said unto Abraham, Thou shalt
keep my covenant therefore, thou, and thy seed after thee in their
__ __ __ __ __ __ __ __ __ __ __. . . . 15 And God
said unto Abraham, As for Sarai thy __ __ __ __, thou shalt
not call her name Sarai, but __ __ __ __ __ shall her name be.
16 And I will bless her, and give thee a son also of her: yea, I will bless
her, and she shall be a __ __ __ __ __ __ of nations; kings

L A U G H E D L M S E R Y G O
N L O P I E G I T C E F R E P
A M O T H E R E V O R E D N O
T I I G N I T S A L R E V E S
I G N S P I S H N G R N I R S
O H E F I W A E I D S E R A E
N T W A R Q U W N T M E A T S
S Y L P I T L U M W O W T I S
D G O I S C H C E A N T H O I
C O V E N A N T E K R E R N O
O D H I L B E C X E X B K S N
N M A H A R B A D G I F A I L
U B C H I R B A C H S R B P E
R E G N A R T S K W A T E I P
E Y L F S G N I K H T P H B A

of people shall be of her. **17** Then Abraham fell upon his face, and
___ ___ ___ ___ ___ ___ ___, and said in his heart, Shall a child be
born unto him that is an ___ ___ ___ ___ ___ ___ ___ years old? and
shall Sarah, that is ninety years old, bear? **18** And Abraham said unto
God, O that Ishmael might live before thee! **19** And God said, Sarah
thy wife shall bear thee a son indeed; and thou shalt call his name
___ ___ ___ ___ ___: and I will establish my covenant with him for an
everlasting covenant, and with his seed after him.

27. JACOB WRESTLES WITH THE ANGEL

Genesis 32:22-31

And [Jacob] rose up that ___ ___ ___ ___ ___, and took his two wives,
and his two ___ ___ ___ ___ ___ ___ ___ ___ ___ ___ ___ ___ ___,
and his eleven sons, and passed over the ford Jabbok. **23** And
he took them, and sent them over the brook, and sent over that
he had. **24** And ___ ___ ___ ___ ___ was left alone; and there
___ ___ ___ ___ ___ ___ ___ ___ a man with him until the
___ ___ ___ ___ ___ ___ ___ ___ of the day. **25** And when he saw that
he ___ ___ ___ ___ ___ ___ ___ ___ ___ not against him, he touched
the hollow of his ___ ___ ___ ___ ___; and the hollow of Jacob's
thigh was ___ ___ ___   ___ ___   ___ ___ ___ ___ ___ (3w),
as he wrestled with him. **26** And he said, ___ ___ ___   ___ ___
___ ___ (3w), for the day breaketh. And he said, I will not let thee go,
except thou ___ ___ ___ ___ ___   ___ ___ (2w). **27** And he said unto
him, What is thy ___ ___ ___ ___? And he said, Jacob. **28** And he said,
Thy name shall be called no more Jacob, but ___ ___ ___ ___ ___ ___:
for as a prince hast thou ___ ___ ___ ___ ___ with God
and with ___ ___ ___, and hast prevailed. **29** And Jacob
___ ___ ___ ___ ___ him, and said, Tell me, ___   ___ ___ ___ ___
___ ___ ___ ___ (3w), thy name. And he said, Wherefore is it that
thou dost ask after my name? And he blessed him there. **30** And Jacob
called the name of the place ___ ___ ___ ___ ___ ___: for I have seen
God ___ ___ ___ ___   ___ ___   ___ ___ ___ ___ (3w), and my
life is ___ ___ ___ ___ ___ ___ ___ ___ ___. **31** And as he passed over
Penuel the ___ ___ ___ rose upon him, and he halted upon his thigh.

```
T G E K E O V H A N O N E R W
V A O R R U Q E U A A T H S H
L S S F L L D S E M S S E L B
E U B A B E T J L E T N O P I
G P R O K Y N H E N N F S M P
F W E S C R I G T G A I I S R
L D A T U A O I M C V S G S A
O E K D S O J H E U R R E H Y
L V I U E K F T G S E A P L T
E R N Y A L O T O E S E U O H
I E G W I F T J D L N L R W E
N S G O A U U S A V E I C P E
E E H C S Q O N E U M A K H N
P R E V A I L E D R O E I R B
L P O F O T E R P O W E R T O
```

28. ELIJAH AND BAAL

1 Kings 18:31-39

And Elijah took twelve __ __ __ __ __ __, according
to the number of the tribes of the __ __ __ __   __ __
__ __ __ __ __ (3w), unto whom the word of the LORD came,
saying, Israel shall be thy name: **32** and with the stones he built
an __ __ __ __ __ in the name of the LORD: and he made a
__ __ __ __ __ __ about the altar, as great as would contain
two measures of seed. **33** And he put the __ __ __ __ in order,
and cut the __ __ __ __ __ __ __ in pieces, and laid him on
the wood, and said, Fill four __ __ __ __ __ __ __ with water,
and pour it on the burnt __ __ __ __ __ __ __ __ __, and
on the wood. **34** And he said, Do it the second time. And they did
it the second time. And he said, Do it the third time. And they did
it the __ __ __ __ __ time. **35** And the water ran round about
the altar; and he filled the trench also with __ __ __ __ __.
36 And it __ __ __ __   __ __   __ __ __ __ (3w)
at the time of the offering of the evening sacrifice, that Elijah the
__ __ __ __ __ __ __ came near, and said, LORD God of
Abraham, __ __ __ __ __, and of Israel, let it be known this
day that thou art God in __ __ __ __ __ __, and that I am thy
__ __ __ __ __ __ __, and that I have done all these things
at thy word. **37** __ __ __ __   __ __ (2w), O LORD, hear
me, that this people may know that thou art the __ __ __ __
__ __ __ (2w), and that thou hast turned their heart back again.
38 Then the __ __ __ __ of the LORD fell, and consumed the
burnt sacrifice, and the wood, and the stones, and the dust, and
__ __ __ __ __ __ up the water that was in the trench. **39** And
when all the people saw it, they fell on their __ __ __ __ __: and
they said, The LORD, he is the God; the LORD, he is the God.

```
U T W L A T I N E W N O I C I
S T O N E S L G O E R C T S H
Q E H P R O E P T N A V R E S
U H C E G N A T D A N E I C A
S P A Y E S R H S E V G N A K
O O M D E O S I L O K K H F A
A R E C I F I R C A S C F M R
U P T M T J T D I T N O I Y E
G R O E O A I P U E A L R L R
A Z P N W C L Q R H N L E O U
N D A M A O H T P E M U C R L
U F S G T B O S A A E B I D A
L A S S E Y V D O R D I T G C
S L E R R A B C K M E P R O L
Y T H F T H K H C E A A G D I
```

29. RAHAB AND THE SPIES

Joshua 2:1, 3-4, 6, 15-17, 18-21

And Joshua the __ __ __ __ __ __ __ __ (3w) sent
out of Shittim two men to __ __ __ secretly, saying, Go view
the land, even __ __ __ __ __ __ __. And they went, and
came into an harlot's house, named Rahab, and lodged there. . . .
3 And the king of Jericho sent unto __ __ __ __ __, saying,
Bring forth the men that are come to thee, which are entered
into thine __ __ __ __ __: for they be come to search out
all the __ __ __ __ __ __ __. **4** And the woman took the
__ __ __ __ __ __ (2w), and hid them. . . . **6** But she had
brought them up to the __ __ __ __ of the house, and hid them
with the stalks of __ __ __ __, which she had laid in order
upon the roof. . . . **15** Then she let them down by a cord through
the __ __ __ __ __ __: for her house was upon the town
__ __ __ __, and she dwelt upon the wall. **16** And she said unto
them, Get you to the __ __ __ __ __ __ __ __, lest the
pursuers meet you; and hide yourselves there __ __ __ __ __
__ __ __ __ (2w), until the pursuers be returned: and
afterward may ye go your way. **17** And the men said unto her. . . .
18 Behold, when we come into the land, thou shalt bind this line of
__ __ __ __ __ __ __ thread in the window which thou didst
let us down by: and thou shalt bring thy father, and thy mother, and thy
brethren, and all thy father's __ __ __ __ __ __ __ __ __,
home unto thee. **19** And it shall be, that whosoever shall go out
of the __ __ __ __ __ of thy house into the street, his
__ __ __ __ __ shall be upon his head, and we will be guiltless:
and whosoever shall be with thee in the house, his blood shall be
on our head, if any hand be upon him. **20** And if thou utter this our

```
I N C E X P P I B K E R I O E
R I S E E O S W D G T O N N V
E A A L W O R D S R A H A B Q
O T T A I A U M E N O C Y L U
M N U G N F L A X U O I I O M
S U C H D A Y L S N B R K O M
H O T T O K I E T F L E T D B
I M O N W C H X P O O J H P U
E N W I O O O N S N Q U R T S
R C G N L U M J H O U S E R I
S T R D D N L E D S P Z E S N
Y H H E O T A V N Y C K D R E
Z E F O O R E A T E L R A C S
B I Y R R Y I G C K S H Y P S
W N T E S O C R H A T M S A G
```

___ ___ ___ ___ ___ ___ ___ ___, then we will be quit of thine oath which thou hast made us to swear. **21** And she said, According unto your ___ ___ ___ ___ ___, so be it. And she sent them away, and they departed: and she bound the scarlet line in the window.

30. THE CROSSING OF THE JORDAN

Joshua 3:5, 14–17

And Joshua said unto the people, __ __ __ __ __ __ __ __
yourselves: for to morrow the LORD will do
__ __ __ __ __ __ __ among you. . . . **14** And it
__ __ __ __   __ __   __ __ __ __ (3w), when the
_ _ _ _ _ _ removed from their __ __ __ __ __, to pass over
Jordan, and the priests bearing the ark __ __   __ __ __
__ __ __ __ __ __ __ __ (3w) before the people; **15** and as
they that bare the ark were come unto __ __ __ __ __ __, and
the feet of the __ __ __ __ __ __ __ that bare the ark were
dipped in the brim of the __ __ __ __ __, (for Jordan overfloweth
all his banks all the time of __ __ __ __ __ __ __,) **16** that
the waters which came down from __ __ __ __ __ stood and
rose up upon an heap very far from the city __ __ __ __, that
is beside Zaretan: and those that came down toward the sea of the
plain, even the __ __ __ __   __ __ __ (2w), failed, and
were cut off: and the people __ __ __ __ __ __ over right
against __ __ __ __ __ __ __. **17** And the priests that bare the
__ __ __ of the covenant of the __ __ __ __ stood firm on
__ __ __   __ __ __ __ __ __ (2w) in the midst of Jordan,
and all the __ __ __ __ __ __ __ __ __ __ passed over on
dry ground, until all the people were passed __ __ __ __ __ over
Jordan.

```
L F W T H E R O L W L H L T C
L O C S E T I L E A R S I E I
B S S R N M E A I T B H I V L
O Y S A M O G H J E O R O O L
H M A R N T N O T R V E A B F
F E P K E C R L C D E S S A P
D R O L S D T E C L H F L V E
R X T O A I N I P P E P N I D
Y G E N D R O O F P N A N H S
G Q M P A T E P W Y I O N A N
R U A O M P R I E S T S B R R
O H C I R E J C H S T T S V T
U R E Y C M B A E L S N H E S
N H H O A E S T L A S B E S B
D O F T H E C O V E N A N T V
```

31. MANNA AND QUAIL FROM HEAVEN

Exodus 16:4, 11-15

Then said the LORD unto Moses, Behold, I will ___ ___ ___ ___
bread from ___ ___ ___ ___ ___ ___ for you; and the people
shall go out and gather a certain rate ___ ___ ___ ___ ___
___ ___ ___ (2w), that I may prove them, whether they will walk
in ___ ___ ___ ___ ___ (2w), or no. . . . 11 And the LORD
spake unto ___ ___ ___ ___ ___, saying, 12 I have heard the
___ ___ ___ ___ ___ ___ ___ ___ ___ ___ of the children of
___ ___ ___ ___ ___ ___: speak unto them, saying, At even ye
shall eat ___ ___ ___ ___ ___, and in the morning ye shall be
filled with ___ ___ ___ ___ ___; and ye shall know that I am the
___ ___ ___ ___ your God. 13 And it ___ ___ ___ ___ ___ ___
___ ___ ___ ___ (3w), that at even the ___ ___ ___ ___ ___ ___
came up, and covered the ___ ___ ___ ___: and in the morning the
dew lay round about the host. 14 And when the ___ ___ ___ that
lay was gone up, ___ ___ ___ ___ ___ ___, upon the face of the
___ ___ ___ ___ ___ ___ ___ ___ ___ ___ there lay a small round
thing, as small as the hoar frost on the ground. 15 And when the
___ ___ ___ ___ ___ ___ ___ ___ of Israel saw it, they said one to
___ ___ ___ ___ ___ ___ ___, It is ___ ___ ___ ___ ___: for they wist
not what it was. And Moses said unto them, This is the bread which
the LORD hath given you to ___ ___ ___.

```
C V T E V E R Y D A Y M C C K
A N H A C K T S E O U E A L B
M O S E S H R Q W A L Y M T T
P A C R A L I H Z K T U E H O
L W H A T V I L I L R O T N I
N I A W T G E A D M S R O F E
J L L H X H S N U R R J P R M
S D N N W A Y R B Q E E A A S
G E R I D T I O O U W N S I S
B R E A D N B E H O L D S N H
K N H T G H I S L L M R T I P
Y E T S S O S P Y O A O A M O
N S O A L J A E S E N L C L W
O S N U P O Y N L H N R L R T
B D A W T I T O L F A E G D E
```

32. ELIJAH AND THE WIDOW

1 Kings 17:7-16

And it came to pass after a while, that the __ __ __ __ __ dried
up, because there had been no rain in the __ __ __ __. **8** And the
__ __ __ __ __ __ __ __ __ __ __ __ (4w)
came unto [Elijah], saying, **9** Arise, get thee to Zarephath, which
belongeth to Zidon, and dwell there: behold, I have commanded a
__ __ __ __ __ woman there to sustain thee. **10** So he arose
and went to __ __ __ __ __ __ __ __ __. And when he
came to the gate of the city, behold, the widow __ __ __ __ __
was there gathering of __ __ __ __ __ __: and he
called to her, and said, Fetch me, I pray thee, a little water in a
__ __ __ __ __ __, that I may __ __ __ __ __. **11** And
as she was going to __ __ __ __ __ it, he called to her, and
said, Bring me, I pray thee, a morsel of __ __ __ __ __ in thine
hand. **12** And she said, As the LORD thy God liveth, I have not a cake,
but an __ __ __ __ __ __ __ of meal in a barrel, and a little
__ __ __ in a cruse: and, behold, I am gathering two sticks, that
I may go in and dress it for me and my son, that we may eat it, and
die. **13** And __ __ __ __ __ __ said unto her, __ __ __ __
__ __ __ (2w); go and do as thou hast said: but make me thereof
a little __ __ __ __ first, and bring it unto me, and after
make for thee and for thy son. **14** For thus saith the LORD God of
__ __ __ __ __ __, The __ __ __ __ __ __ of meal shall
not waste, neither shall the __ __ __ __ __ of oil fail, until the
day that the LORD sendeth __ __ __ __ upon the earth. **15** And she
went and did according to the saying of Elijah: and she, and he, and
her __ __ __ __ __, did eat many days. **16** And the barrel of meal
__ __ __ __ __ __ __ __ __ (2w), neither did the cruse of
oil fail, according to the word of the LORD, which he spake by Elijah.

A	M	D	R	O	L	E	H	T	F	O	D	R	O	W
L	L	N	S	S	N	T	A	C	H	K	Y	H	M	A
L	A	A	S	T	K	O	N	S	R	P	S	O	M	S
N	W	L	O	I	O	N	D	A	H	O	C	K	R	T
K	U	F	H	C	T	E	F	K	D	U	Z	C	A	E
N	M	C	A	K	E	S	U	E	O	A	C	L	S	D
I	R	P	I	S	E	U	L	L	R	O	H	U	I	N
R	H	L	H	E	L	O	A	E	H	Y	R	N	D	O
D	N	N	S	G	I	H	P	S	A	C	O	B	W	T
A	R	S	Y	E	J	H	B	A	M	R	Q	U	T	O
E	H	N	K	N	A	D	A	N	C	E	S	W	H	N
R	S	L	T	T	H	L	R	W	A	K	H	I	B	R
B	N	N	H	P	P	F	R	D	U	M	A	D	N	A
A	O	N	G	T	O	O	E	N	O	R	O	O	D	E
A	G	V	E	S	S	E	L	R	A	I	N	W	P	F

33. JONAH

Jonah 2

Then Jonah prayed unto the LORD his God out of the fish's
__ __ __ __ __, **2** and said, I cried by reason of mine
__ __ __ __ __ __ __ __ __ __ unto the LORD, and
he heard me; out of the belly of hell cried I, and thou heardest my
voice. **3** For thou hadst cast me __ __ __ __   __ __ __
__ __ __ __ (3w), in the midst of the seas; and the
__ __ __ __ __ __ compassed me about: all thy billows and thy
__ __ __ __ __ passed over me. **4** Then I said, I am cast out of thy
__ __ __ __ __; yet I will look again toward thy __ __ __ __
__ __ __ __ __ __ (2w). **5** The waters compassed me about,
even to the soul: the __ __ __ __ __ closed me round about,
the __ __ __ __ __ were wrapped about my head. **6** I went
down to the bottoms of the __ __ __ __ __ __ __ __ __;
the earth with her bars was about me for ever: yet hast thou brought
up my life from corruption, __   __ __ __ __   __ __
__ __ __ (4w). **7** When my soul __ __ __ __ __ __ __ __
within me I __ __ __ __ __ __ __ __ __ __ the LORD:
and my __ __ __ __ __ __ came in unto thee, into thine holy
temple. **8** They that observe lying __ __ __ __ __ __ __ __
forsake their own __ __ __ __ __. **9** But I will sacrifice unto thee
with the voice of __ __ __ __ __ __ __ __ __ __ __ __; I
will pay that that I have vowed. __ __ __ __ __ __ __ __ __
is of the LORD. **10** And the LORD spake unto the fish, and it
__ __ __ __ __ __ __ out Jonah upon the __ __ __
__ __ __ __ (2w).

```
O  L  A  E  W  R  L  B  S  D  E  E  W  S  N
S  A  L  V  A  T  I  O  N  E  N  N  P  E  O
E  F  E  N  V  I  O  S  R  R  M  I  S  I  I
I  F  P  C  E  U  N  N  A  E  B  L  E  L  V
T  L  H  H  S  L  L  I  R  B  E  P  S  P  O
I  I  N  T  Q  U  S  C  G  M  L  P  D  E  M
N  C  C  P  R  A  Y  E  R  E  L  E  O  E  I
A  T  A  E  O  L  O  R  D  M  Y  G  O  D  T
V  I  D  D  H  O  L  Y  T  E  M  P  L  E  E
I  O  R  P  S  D  N  S  A  R  O  O  F  H  D
N  N  Y  P  F  A  I  N  T  E  D  C  H  T  V
G  B  L  G  O  G  S  N  I  A  T  N  U  O  M
T  B  A  K  H  N  V  A  D  V  A  G  A  T  I
E  L  N  T  H  A  N  K  S  G  I  V  I  N  G
O  A  D  R  T  C  K  Q  U  S  R  K  E  I  N
```

34. PARABLE OF THE TALENTS

Matthew 25:14-15, 19-29

For the kingdom of ___ ___ ___ ___ ___ ___ is as a man travelling into a far country, who called his own servants, and delivered unto them his goods. **15** And unto one he gave five ___ ___ ___ ___ ___ ___ ___, to another two, and to another one; to every man according to his several ability; and straightway took his ___ ___ ___ ___ ___ ___ ___. . . . **19** After a long time the lord of those servants cometh, and reckoneth with them. **20** And so he that had received five talents came and brought other five talents, saying, ___ ___ ___ ___, thou deliveredst unto me five talents: behold, I have gained beside them ___ ___ ___ ___ talents more. **21** His lord said unto him, Well done, thou good and faithful servant: thou hast been ___ ___ ___ ___ ___ ___ ___ over a few things, I will make thee ruler over ___ ___ ___ ___ ___ ___ ___ ___ ___ ___ (2w): enter thou into the joy of thy lord. **22** He also that had received two talents came and said, Lord, thou deliveredst unto me two talents: behold, I have gained two other talents beside them. **23** His lord said unto him, Well done, good and faithful ___ ___ ___ ___ ___ ___ ___; thou hast been faithful over a few things, I will make thee ___ ___ ___ ___ ___ over many things: enter thou into the ___ ___ ___ ___ ___ ___ ___ ___ ___ ___ ___ (4w). **24** Then he which had ___ ___ ___ ___ ___ ___ ___ ___ the one talent came and said, Lord, I knew thee that thou art an ___ ___ ___ ___ man, reaping where thou hast not ___ ___ ___ ___, and gathering where thou hast not strawed: **25** and I was ___ ___ ___ ___ ___ ___, and went and hid thy talent in the ___ ___ ___ ___ ___: lo, there thou hast that is thine. **26** His lord answered and said unto him, Thou ___ ___ ___ ___ ___ ___ and slothful servant, thou knewest that

```
L  I  S  G  N  I  H  T  Y  N  A  M  G  C  T
K  Y  E  N  R  U  O  J  E  E  A  R  T  H  E
E  H  B  T  R  E  R  O  N  S  B  N  N  E  F
G  O  X  A  A  T  C  Y  O  T  U  L  N  X  A
E  L  H  K  F  H  S  O  M  N  N  O  L  C  I
R  U  L  E  R  A  H  F  S  E  D  R  J  H  T
E  G  P  N  A  D  O  T  W  L  A  D  R  A  H
C  A  M  A  I  Q  H  H  B  A  N  S  C  N  F
E  L  O  W  D  U  N  Y  Y  T  C  E  H  G  U
I  J  N  A  M  Y  W  L  A  U  E  R  D  E  L
V  I  E  Y  M  H  O  O  J  V  O  V  D  R  E
E  N  V  F  E  N  S  R  S  B  E  A  X  S  O
D  G  W  I  C  K  E  D  P  P  G  N  L  L  O
B  N  I  V  H  C  G  V  E  N  R  T  I  J  N
E  G  L  E  Z  S  O  D  E  N  E  V  A  E  H
```

I reap where I sowed not, and gather where I have not strawed:
27 thou oughtest therefore to have put my ___ ___ ___ ___ ___
to the ___ ___ ___ ___ ___ ___ ___ ___ ___ ___, and then at my
coming I should have received mine own with usury. **28** Take therefore
the talent from him, and give it unto him which hath ten talents.
29 For unto every one that hath shall be given, and he shall have

___ ___ ___ ___ ___ ___ ___ ___ ___: but from him that hath not
shall be ___ ___ ___ ___ ___ ___ ___ ___ ___ (2w) even that which
he hath.

35. PARABLE OF THE SOWER

Matthew 13:3-9, 18-23

Behold, a sower went forth to sow; **4** and when he

__ __ __ __ __, some seeds fell by the way side, and the

__ __ __ __ __ came and devoured them up: **5** some fell

upon __ __ __ __ __   __ __ __ __ __ __ (2w),

where they had not much earth: and forthwith they

__ __ __ __ __ __   __ __ (2w), because they had no

deepness of __ __ __ __ __: **6** and when the sun was up, they

were __ __ __ __ __ __ __ __; and because they had no root,

they __ __ __ __ __ __ __ __ away. **7** And some fell among

thorns; and the thorns sprung up, and __ __ __ __ __ __ them:

8 but other fell into good __ __ __ __ __ __, and brought

forth __ __ __ __ __, some an hundredfold, some sixtyfold,

some thirtyfold. **9** Who hath ears to hear, let him hear. . . . **18** Hear

ye therefore the parable of the sower. **19** When any one heareth the

word of the __ __ __ __ __ __ __, and understandeth it not,

then cometh the __ __ __ __ __ __ __   __ __ __ (2w),

and catcheth away that which was sown in his heart. This is he

which received __ __ __ __ by the way side. **20** But he that

received the seed into stony places, the same is he that heareth

the word, and anon with __ __ __ receiveth it; **21** yet hath he

not __ __ __ __ in himself, but dureth for a while: for when

__ __ __ __ __ __ __ __ __ __ __ or persecution ariseth

because of the word, by and by he is __ __ __ __ __ __ __ __.

22 He also that received seed among the thorns is he that heareth

the word; and the care of this world, and the deceitfulness of

__ __ __ __ __ __, choke the word, and he becometh

__ __ __ __ __ __ __ __ __. **23** But he that received

```
W  I  T  H  E  R  E  D  E  H  C  R  O  C  S
S  I  R  O  P  S  C  H  O  K  E  D  T  H  S
L  T  I  N  G  G  S  L  W  O  F  K  O  H  E
U  S  E  R  I  O  D  E  D  N  E  F  F  O  C
F  P  K  I  S  H  E  H  W  O  F  V  G  I  A
T  R  I  B  U  L  A  T  I  O  N  S  H  J  L
I  U  O  S  S  L  R  P  C  V  F  G  N  N  P
U  N  J  O  Y  J  T  P  K  R  R  R  M  R  Y
R  G  S  W  T  A  H  N  E  K  H  O  U  R  N
F  U  H  E  S  M  M  Y  D  C  D  U  T  I  O
N  P  C  D  E  E  S  S  O  G  G  N  H  C  T
U  U  L  W  S  S  I  H  N  R  L  D  W  H  S
I  F  P  B  E  O  R  I  E  B  E  L  S  E  E
G  J  V  N  N  O  K  Y  V  A  P  P  V  S  R
H  U  N  D  R  E  D  F  O  L  D  T  I  O  N
```

seed into the good ground is he that heareth the word, and understandeth it; which also beareth fruit, and bringeth forth, some an __ __ __ __ __ __ __ __ __ __ __, some sixty, some thirty.

36. PARABLE OF THE PRODIGAL SON

Luke 15:11-24

And he said, A certain man had ___ ___ ___ ___ ___ ___ ___ (2w):
12 and the younger of them said to his father, ___ ___ ___ ___ ___ ___,
give me the portion of goods that falleth to me. And he
divided unto them his living. **13** And not many days after the
___ ___ ___ ___ ___ ___ ___ son gathered all together, and
took his ___ ___ ___ ___ ___ ___ ___ into a far country, and
there wasted his substance with ___ ___ ___ ___ ___ ___ ___
___ ___ ___ ___ ___ ___ (2w). **14** And when he had spent all, there
arose a mighty ___ ___ ___ ___ ___ ___ in that land; and he began
to ___ ___ ___ ___ ___ ___ ___ ___ (3w). **15** And he went and
joined himself to a citizen of that country; and he sent him into his
fields to feed ___ ___ ___ ___ ___. **16** And he would fain have filled
his ___ ___ ___ ___ ___ with the husks that the swine did eat: and no
man gave unto him. **17** And when he came to himself, he said, How
many hired ___ ___ ___ ___ ___ ___ ___ ___ of my father's have
bread enough and to spare, and I perish with ___ ___ ___ ___ ___ ___!
18 I will arise and go to my father, and will say unto him, Father,
I have sinned against ___ ___ ___ ___ ___ ___, and before thee,
19 and am no more worthy to be called thy son: make me as one of
thy ___ ___ ___ ___ ___ servants. **20** And he arose, and came to his
father. But when he was yet a great way off, his father saw him, and
had ___ ___ ___ ___ ___ ___ ___ ___ ___ ___, and ran, and fell
on his neck, and ___ ___ ___ ___ ___ ___ him. **21** And the son said
unto him, Father, I have sinned against heaven, and in thy sight, and
am no more worthy to be ___ ___ ___ ___ ___ ___ ___ ___ ___
___ ___ ___ (3w). **22** But the father said to his servants, Bring forth the
best ___ ___ ___ ___, and put it on him; and put a ___ ___ ___ ___

```
G  R  E  H  T  A  F  L  A  C  T  F  O  J  N
D  J  O  U  R  N  E  Y  O  U  N  G  E  R  N
B  L  R  O  L  S  E  A  R  T  H  N  M  O  C
P  S  A  C  M  S  T  N  A  W  N  I  E  B  E
I  P  M  A  O  V  C  E  J  O  F  V  R  E  R
Y  H  B  L  B  M  K  B  R  S  R  I  R  E  V
I  R  P  L  M  H  P  E  M  O  U  L  Y  O  D
T  H  T  E  J  E  G  A  U  N  L  S  Q  U  E
F  E  W  D  E  N  H  H  S  S  L  U  S  B  S
E  P  O  T  U  T  P  E  R  S  F  O  S  B  S
N  H  S  H  E  A  V  E  N  N  I  T  W  A  I
I  N  L  Y  L  L  E  B  J  P  P  O  I  O  K
M  A  I  S  E  R  V  A  N  T  S  I  N  L  P
A  E  R  O  A  J  O  I  G  N  I  R  E  L  E
F  O  U  N  D  L  P  C  E  Y  H  C  U  Y  R
```

on his hand, and shoes on his ___ ___ ___ ___: **23** and bring
hither the fatted ___ ___ ___ ___, and kill it; and let us eat, and be
___ ___ ___ ___ ___: **24** for this my son was dead, and is alive again;
he was lost, and is ___ ___ ___ ___ ___. And they began to be merry.

37. JESUS HEALS MANY

Luke 8:43-48; 17:11-19

And a woman having an __ __ __ __ __ __ __
__ __ __ __ __ (3w) twelve years, which had spent all her
living upon __ __ __ __ __ __ __ __ __ __, neither
could be healed of any, **44** came behind him, and touched the
border of his __ __ __ __ __ __ __: and immediately
her issue of blood stanched. **45** And Jesus said, __ __ __
__ __ __ __ __ __ __ __ (3w)? When all denied,
Peter and they that were with him said, __ __ __ __ __ __,
the multitude throng thee and press thee, and sayest thou, Who
touched me? **46** And Jesus said, __ __ __ __ __ __ __ __
hath touched me: for I perceive that __ __ __ __ __ __ is
gone out of me. **47** And when the __ __ __ __ __ saw that
she was not hid, she came __ __ __ __ __ __ __ __ __,
and falling down before him, she declared unto him before all
the people for what cause she had touched him, and how she
was __ __ __ __ __ __ immediately. **48** And he said unto
her, __ __ __ __ __ __ __ __, be of good comfort:
thy faith hath made thee whole; go in peace. . . **11** And it came
to pass, as he went to Jerusalem, that he passed through the
midst of Samaria and __ __ __ __ __ __ __. **12** And as
he entered into a certain village, there met him ten men that
were __ __ __ __ __ __, which stood afar off: **13** and
they lifted up their __ __ __ __ __ __, and said, Jesus,
Master, have __ __ __ __ __ on us. **14** And when he
saw them, he said unto them, Go shew yourselves unto the
__ __ __ __ __ __ __. And it came to pass, that, as they
went, they were __ __ __ __ __ __ __ __. **15** And one of

```
C A T G N I L B M E R T H V O
H K S O M E B O D Y S G E Y L
C E N R A I E S C R S W L E G
L S A S N U T R N O C H O P T
E H I S T L E P N L H O H P S
A X C R L M S H O G V T W I T
N W I S S U E O F B L O O D R
S V S G G A R M E N T U M A A
E O Y Q M Y D E Q U J C A U N
D I H U M W E L T K C H N G G
E C P R I E S T S S K E N H E
L E P E R S C E P P A D G T R
A S T I O N I G N I Z M H E K
E O L J D D G A L I L E E R L
H T I A F V O M A X N N N J A
```

them, when he saw that he was healed, turned back, and with a loud voice glorified God, **16** and fell down on his face at his feet, giving him thanks: and he was a Samaritan. **17** And Jesus answering said, Were there not ten cleansed? but where are the ___ ___ ___ ___?
18 There are not found that returned to give ___ ___ ___ ___ ___ to God, save this ___ ___ ___ ___ ___ ___ ___ ___. **19** And he said unto him, Arise, go thy way: thy ___ ___ ___ ___ ___ hath made thee ___ ___ ___ ___ ___.

38. THE HOLY SPIRIT ARRIVES

Acts 2:1–8, 12–21

And when the day of ___ ___ ___ ___ ___ ___ ___ ___ ___ was fully come, they were all with one accord in one place. **2** And suddenly there came a sound from heaven as of a rushing ___ ___ ___ ___ ___ ___ ___ ___ ___ ___ (2w), and it filled all the house where they were sitting. **3** And there appeared unto them cloven tongues like as of ___ ___ ___ ___, and it sat upon each of them. **4** And they were all filled with the ___ ___ ___ ___ ___ ___ ___ ___ ___ (2w), and began to speak with other ___ ___ ___ ___ ___ ___ ___, as the Spirit gave them utterance. **5** And there were dwelling at Jerusalem Jews, devout men, out of every nation under ___ ___ ___ ___ ___ ___.
6 Now when this was noised abroad, the multitude came together, and were confounded, because that every man heard them speak in his own ___ ___ ___ ___ ___ ___ ___ ___. **7** And they were all amazed and marvelled, saying one to another, Behold, are not all these which speak Galilaeans? **8** And how hear we every man in our own tongue, wherein we were ___ ___ ___ ___? . . . **12** And they were all amazed, and were in ___ ___ ___ ___ ___, saying one to another, What meaneth this? **13** Others ___ ___ ___ ___ ___ ___ ___ said, These men are full of new wine. **14** But Peter, standing up with the ___ ___ ___ ___ ___ ___, lifted up his voice, and said unto them, Ye men of ___ ___ ___ ___ ___ ___, and all ye that dwell at Jerusalem, be this known unto you, and hearken to my words:
15 for these are not ___ ___ ___ ___ ___ ___ ___, as ye suppose, seeing it is but the third hour of the day. **16** But this is that which was spoken by the prophet Joel; **17** And it shall come to pass in the ___ ___ ___ ___ ___ ___ ___ ___ (2w), saith God, I will pour out of my ___ ___ ___ ___ ___ ___ upon all flesh: and your sons and your

```
E  I  T  O  N  G  U  E  S  A  C  O  S  P  L
A  P  L  K  E  E  E  R  K  C  P  H  S  D  S
N  F  D  E  V  A  S  E  B  H  S  T  R  O  N
E  Y  H  R  A  F  R  M  Y  V  S  E  T  U  D
V  S  A  E  E  H  L  A  A  O  G  S  H  B  G
E  E  N  T  H  P  G  V  C  E  O  Y  Y  T  O
L  D  D  O  O  L  B  E  L  L  R  A  S  J  O
E  P  M  I  G  H  T  Y  W  I  N  D  E  U  R
G  F  A  L  L  N  K  B  R  O  E  T  G  D  T
A  F  I  R  E  E  E  E  O  T  I  S  N  A  T
U  Z  D  P  T  K  Y  M  L  R  V  A  I  E  H
G  Y  E  X  O  P  P  A  I  K  N  L  K  A  A
N  N  N  M  N  C  K  P  R  L  G  P  C  G  G
A  T  S  L  P  T  S  O  H  G  Y  L  O  H  N
L  K  I  D  R  U  N  K  E  N  N  N  M  H  C
```

daughters shall prophesy, and your young men shall see visions, and
your old men shall dream __ __ __ __ __ __: **18** and on my
servants and on my __ __ __ __ __ __ __ __ __ __ __ __
I will pour out in those days of my Spirit; and they shall prophesy:
19 and I will shew wonders in heaven above, and signs in the
earth beneath; __ __ __ __ __, and fire, and vapour of
__ __ __ __ __: **20** the sun shall be turned into darkness, and the
__ __ __ __ into blood, before the great and notable day of the
Lord come: **21** and it shall come to pass, that whosoever shall call on
the name of the Lord shall __ __   __ __ __ __ __ (2w).

39. JESUS' BIRTH

Luke 2:1-20

And it came to pass in those days, that there went out a

__ __ __ __ __ __ from Caesar Augustus that all the world

should be taxed. **2** (And this taxing was first made when Cyrenius was

governor of Syria.) **3** And all went to be __ __ __ __ __, every

one into his own city. **4** And __ __ __ __ __ __ also went up

from Galilee, out of the city of __ __ __ __ __ __ __ __, into

Judaea, unto the city of David, which is called Bethlehem; (because he

was of the house and lineage of __ __ __ __ __:) **5** to be taxed

with Mary his espoused wife, being great with __ __ __ __ __.

6 And so it was, that, while they were there, the days were

accomplished that she should be delivered. **7** And she brought forth

her __ __ __ __ __ __ __ __ __ son, and wrapped him

in swaddling clothes, and laid him in a __ __ __ __ __ __;

because there was no room for them in the __ __ __. **8** And there

were in the same country shepherds abiding in the field, keeping

watch over their __ __ __ __ __ by night. **9** And, lo, the angel

of the Lord came upon them, and the glory of the Lord shone round

about them: and they were sore __ __ __ __ __ __. **10** And

the angel said unto them, __ __ __ __ __ __ __ (2w): for,

behold, I bring you good tidings of great joy, which shall be to all

__ __ __ __ __ __. **11** For unto you is born this day in the city

of David a __ __ __ __ __ __ __, which is Christ the Lord.

12 And this shall be a sign unto you; Ye shall find the babe wrapped

in swaddling __ __ __ __ __ __ __, lying in a manger.

13 And suddenly there was with the angel a multitude of the heavenly

__ __ __ __ praising God, and saying, **14** __ __ __ __ __ to

God in the highest, and on earth peace, good will toward men. **15** And

it came to pass, as the angels were gone away from them into heaven,

N	L	P	E	P	R	N	H	J	M	M	S	F	I	E
O	A	J	O	R	D	A	V	I	D	D	S	H	N	J
I	E	R	K	T	P	Z	F	N	O	L	A	T	P	G
T	B	E	A	S	N	A	W	R	W	N	I	O	Z	H
S	A	V	I	O	U	R	K	E	A	K	Q	H	T	K
N	B	E	T	H	L	E	H	E	M	I	U	U	C	T
N	A	Z	F	Y	W	T	E	L	G	O	D	O	L	S
S	G	W	I	J	J	H	A	L	U	G	L	E	O	F
F	E	A	R	N	O	T	R	X	D	F	O	S	T	H
R	K	O	S	X	S	R	T	A	E	H	T	G	H	P
L	D	I	T	R	E	E	R	C	E	D	G	L	E	P
O	L	N	B	L	P	A	C	Y	S	J	O	O	S	H
E	A	N	O	T	H	E	R	D	H	R	P	R	A	N
K	I	W	R	H	W	A	L	X	D	L	T	Y	Z	G
R	E	G	N	A	M	C	H	U	E	L	H	I	C	K

the shepherds said one to __ __ __ __ __ __ __, Let us now
go even unto __ __ __ __ __ __ __ __ __, and see this
thing which is come to pass, which the Lord hath made known unto
us. **16** And they came with haste, and found __ __ __ __,
and Joseph, and the __ __ __ __ lying in a manger. **17** And when
they had seen it, they made known abroad the saying which was told
them concerning this child. **18** And all they that heard it wondered
at those things which were told them by the shepherds. **19** But Mary
kept all these things, and pondered them in her __ __ __ __ __.
20 And the shepherds returned, glorifying and praising __ __ __ for
all the things that they had heard and seen, as it was __ __ __ __
unto them.

40. JESUS DEDICATED AT THE TEMPLE

Luke 2:25-39

25 And, behold, there was a man in Jerusalem, whose name was __ __ __ __ __ __; and the same man was just and __ __ __ __ __ __, waiting for the consolation of Israel: and the __ __ __ __ __ __ __ __ __ (2w) was upon him. **26** And it was revealed unto him by the Holy Ghost, that he should not see death, before he had seen the Lord's __ __ __ __ __ __. **27** And he came by the Spirit into the temple: and when the __ __ __ __ __ __ __ brought in the child Jesus, to do for him after the custom of the __ __ __, **28** then took he him up in his arms, and blessed God, and said, **29** Lord, now lettest thou thy servant depart in peace, according to thy word: **30** for mine eyes have seen thy __ __ __ __ __ __ __ __ __, **31** which thou hast prepared before the face of all people; **32** a light to lighten the Gentiles, and the glory of thy people __ __ __ __ __ __. **33** And Joseph and his mother marvelled at those things which were spoken of him. **34** And Simeon blessed them, and said unto __ __ __ __ his mother, Behold, this __ __ __ __ __ is set for the fall and rising again of many in Israel; and for a sign which shall be spoken against; **35** (yea, a sword shall pierce through thy own __ __ __ __ also,) that the thoughts of many hearts may be __ __ __ __ __ __ __ __. **36** And there was one __ __ __ __, a prophetess, the daughter of Phanuel, of the tribe of Aser: she was of a great age, and had lived with an __ __ __ __ __ __ __ seven years from her virginity; **37** and she was a __ __ __ __ __ of about fourscore and four years, which departed not from the __ __ __ __ __ __, but served God with fastings and __ __ __ __ __ __ __ night and day. **38** And she coming in that instant gave __ __ __ __ __ __

```
N E L T I O N P K C J A C T H
L R C H I L D N A B S U H D O
E E I G G G L S H K W R R W L
H Q U L R Y K M N P S N I P Y
R F I I A N N A A P R N S H G
E Y S N S U H A Y R E D T K H
V D R M I T N G Z X Y E W E O
E N A Y M S N O I T A V L A S
A K E I E H P E L K R O S G T
L E L N O W P T R L P U D X H
E L L G N S I O E A J T D G S
D S E X K R E D E M P T I O N
R U A N M M C D O A P K U C E
R K E G L J L H T W A L K W R
Y E S A I O G A L I L E E P P
```

likewise unto the Lord, and spake of him to all them that looked for
___ ___ ___ ___ ___ ___ ___ ___ ___ ___ in Jerusalem. **39** And
when they had performed all things according to the law of the Lord,
they returned into ___ ___ ___ ___ ___ ___ ___, to their own city
Nazareth.

41. THE WISE MEN

Matthew 2:1-12

Now when Jesus was born in Bethlehem of __ __ __ __ __ __
in the days of __ __ __ __ __ the king, behold, there came wise
men from the east to Jerusalem, **2** saying, Where is he that is born
__ __ __ __   __ __   __ __ __   __ __ __ __ (4w)?
for we have seen his __ __ __ __ in the __ __ __ __,
and are come to worship him. **3** When Herod the king had heard
these things, he was __ __ __ __ __ __ __ __, and all
Jerusalem with him. **4** And when he had gathered all the chief
__ __ __ __ __ __ __ and scribes of the people together,
he demanded of them where __ __ __ __ __ __ should
be born. **5** And they said unto him, In Bethlehem of Judaea: for
thus it is written by the __ __ __ __ __ __ __, **6** and
thou Bethlehem, in the land of Juda, art not the least among the
__ __ __ __ __ __ __ of Juda: for out of thee shall come a
Governor, that shall __ __ __ __ my people Israel. **7** Then Herod,
when he had privily called the __ __ __ __   __ __ __ (2w),
enquired of them diligently what time the star appeared. **8** And he
sent them to Bethlehem, and said, Go and search diligently for the
young child; and when ye have found him, bring me word again, that
I may come and __ __ __ __ __ __ __ him also. **9** When
they had heard the king, they departed; and, lo, the star, which
they saw in the east, went before them, till it came and stood over
where the __ __ __ __ __ child was. **10** When they saw the
star, they __ __ __ __ __ __ __ __ with exceeding great
joy. **11** And when they were come into the __ __ __ __ __,
they saw the young child with __ __ __ __ his mother, and
fell down, and worshipped him: and when they had opened their

```
C A M Y R R H R E P M O O S A
T T W O R S H I P S P R I N P
S E R U S A E R T W R E Y V N
I H R N E E X A R E I P E O W
R P V G H I R R O J N K L N Y
H O U S E R B E U E C P G K G
C R A M A E R D B H E R O D R
H P M O D U A S L T S I L E O
N E R O L E V H E F J E D C Q
N W D E A U Y A D O R S T I U
A V D W T J R K N G Z T I O G
Q W N P P E A S T N T S O J M
U J E T N E M E S I W H N E M
R W M N N Y L E N K D P W R A
W Y I N G O N V N O H T J E R
```

___ ___ ___ ___ ___ ___ ___ ___ ___, they presented unto him gifts; ___ ___ ___ ___, and frankincense and ___ ___ ___ ___ ___. **12** And being warned of God in a ___ ___ ___ ___ ___ that they should not return to Herod, they departed into their own country another way.

42. JESUS TEACHES AT THE TEMPLE

Luke 2:40-52

And the child ___ ___ ___ ___, and waxed strong in spirit, filled with

___ ___ ___ ___ ___ ___: and the grace of God was upon him. **41** Now

his ___ ___ ___ ___ ___ ___ ___ went to Jerusalem every year at

the feast of the ___ ___ ___ ___ ___ ___ ___ ___. **42** And when he

was ___ ___ ___ ___ ___ ___ years old, they went up to Jerusalem

after the custom of the feast. **43** And when they had fulfilled the days,

as they returned, the child Jesus tarried behind in Jerusalem; and

___ ___ ___ ___ ___ ___ and his mother knew not of it. **44** But they,

supposing him to have been in the company, went a day's journey;

and they sought him among their ___ ___ ___ ___ ___ ___ ___ ___

and acquaintance. **45** And when they found him not, they turned

back again to ___ ___ ___ ___ ___ ___ ___ ___ ___, seeking him.

46 And it ___ ___ ___ ___ ___ ___ ___ ___ ___ ___ (3w), that

after three days they found him in the ___ ___ ___ ___ ___ ___,

sitting in the midst of the doctors, both hearing them, and asking

them questions. **47** And all that heard him were astonished at his

___ ___ ___ ___ ___ ___ ___ ___ ___ ___ ___ ___ ___ and answers.

48 And when they saw him, they were ___ ___ ___ ___ ___ ___:

and his mother said unto him, ___ ___ ___, why hast thou thus

dealt with us? behold, thy ___ ___ ___ ___ ___ ___ and I have

sought thee sorrowing. **49** And he said unto them, How is it

that ye sought me? wist ye not that I must be about my Father's

___ ___ ___ ___ ___ ___ ___ ___? **50** And they understood not the

saying which he spake unto them. **51** And he went down with them,

and came to ___ ___ ___ ___ ___ ___ ___ ___, and was subject

unto them: but his ___ ___ ___ ___ ___ ___ kept all these sayings

in her ___ ___ ___ ___ ___. **52** And Jesus increased in wisdom

I	P	T	A	L	I	O	N	S	H	X	N	G	P	W
N	E	J	E	S	S	E	N	I	S	U	B	D	L	O
G	T	W	E	L	V	E	M	A	R	H	D	D	J	N
N	P	K	I	N	S	F	O	L	K	T	H	S	E	M
I	A	R	T	S	P	Q	U	L	T	E	W	E	R	G
D	R	V	O	E	D	I	J	C	L	R	D	J	U	E
N	E	N	E	Z	N	O	H	P	J	A	P	E	S	M
A	N	I	L	N	S	A	M	D	E	Z	A	M	A	D
T	T	W	S	E	N	E	R	X	O	A	S	O	L	D
S	S	A	P	O	T	E	M	A	C	N	S	M	E	V
R	W	H	E	A	R	T	O	E	M	P	O	L	M	E
E	R	E	R	U	T	A	T	S	K	E	V	T	C	H
D	T	P	P	X	O	F	H	A	C	U	E	L	Z	I
N	A	M	L	L	K	O	E	F	L	B	R	F	R	G
U	B	R	E	A	N	N	R	E	H	T	A	F	A	H

and __ __ __ __ __ __ __, and in favour with God and
__ __ __.

43. JESUS TURNS WATER INTO WINE

John 2:1-11

And the third day there was a __ __ __ __ __ __ __ __
in Cana of Galilee; and the mother of Jesus was there: **2** and
both __ __ __ __ __ was called, and his disciples, to
the marriage. **3** And when they wanted __ __ __ __, the
__ __ __ __ __ __ of Jesus saith unto him, They have no wine.
4 Jesus saith unto her, __ __ __ __ __, what have I to do with
thee? mine hour is not yet come. **5** His mother saith unto the servants,
Whatsoever he saith unto you, __ __   __ __ (2w). **6** And there
were set there __ __ __ waterpots of __ __ __ __ __, after
the manner of the __ __ __ __ __ __ __ __ __ of the Jews,
containing two or three firkins apiece. **7** Jesus saith unto them, Fill
the waterpots with __ __ __ __ __. And they filled them up
to the __ __ __ __. **8** And he saith unto them, Draw out now,
and bear unto the governor of the __ __ __ __ __. And they
bare it. **9** When the __ __ __ __ __ of the feast had tasted the
water that was made wine, and knew not whence it was: (but the
__ __ __ __ __ __ __ __ which drew the water knew;) the
__ __ __ __ __ __ __ __ of the feast called the bridegroom,
10 and saith unto him, Every man at the beginning doth set forth good
wine; and when men have well __ __ __ __ __, then that which
is worse: but thou hast kept the good wine until now. **11** This beginning
of __ __ __ __ __ __ __ __ did Jesus in __ __ __ __
of Galilee, and manifested forth his __ __ __ __ __; and his
disciples __ __ __ __ __ __ __ __ on him.

```
P I N R A L A W E E J U P A Y
L W C Y W I J Z K R E L U R J
L B E L I E V E D E A Y R E L
R X M B S N Q W E N E E I B X
G M K U O I Y U A E H O F Y U
Y C S E X W D C R T J O Y B E
S S T I C H O G O W E B I I E
Y R O L G T I M I S H R N N K
I J N I I Y T A A T Q I G G F
N F E A S T N R C N U M K O W
G L L E X S R E A R N T O T
E C H S K A J I H V U S C K I
K R E H W C H A X R T H B T O
R O N R E V O G D E Z B J Y N
W M I R A C L E S S W O U O H
```

44. JESUS CALLS SIMON PETER

Luke 5:1-11

And it came to pass, that, as the people pressed upon him to hear the
___ ___ ___ ___ ___ ___ ___ ___ ___ (3w), he stood by the lake
of Gennesaret, **2** and saw two ___ ___ ___ ___ ___ standing by the
lake: but the fishermen were gone out of them, and were washing their
___ ___ ___ ___. **3** And he entered into one of the ships, which was
Simon's, and ___ ___ ___ ___ ___ ___ him that he would thrust out
a little from the land. And he sat down, and ___ ___ ___ ___ ___ ___
the people out of the ship. **4** Now when he had left speaking, he said
unto ___ ___ ___ ___ ___, Launch out into the ___ ___ ___ ___,
and let down your nets for a draught. **5** And Simon answering said
unto him, ___ ___ ___ ___ ___ ___, we have toiled all the night,
and have taken ___ ___ ___ ___ ___ ___ ___: nevertheless at thy
word I will let down the net. **6** And when they had this done, they
inclosed a great multitude of ___ ___ ___ ___ ___ ___: and their
net brake. **7** And they beckoned unto their partners, which were in
the other ship, that they should come and ___ ___ ___ ___ them.
And they came, and ___ ___ ___ ___ ___ ___ both the ships, so that
they began to ___ ___ ___ ___. **8** When Simon _ _ _ _ _ saw it, he
fell down at Jesus' knees, saying, Depart from me; for I am a sinful
man, ___ ___ ___ ___ ___ (2w). **9** For he was astonished, and
all that were with him, at the draught of the fishes which they had
taken: **10** and so was also James, and ___ ___ ___ ___, the sons of
Zebedee, which were partners with Simon. And ___ ___ ___ ___ ___
said unto Simon, ___ ___ ___ ___ ___ ___ ___ (2w); from
henceforth thou shalt catch ___ ___ ___. **11** And when they had
brought their ships to ___ ___ ___ ___, they forsook all, and
___ ___ ___ ___ ___ ___ ___ ___ him.

```
L M L A N D E W O L L O F O L
E S I S W R E O X E D A E P H
B J H S B P V R E T E P A B D
I R F I L L E D C R E W R R O
K E G N I H T O N E P O N L O
A O F K N G S F S S I M O N J
Y P N O O U I G W G A R T T I
T L H Z S H K O N S D M A M Y
I X O E Z T E D H M W E U E E
O A J W O A E N E M A L G L M
N M S P M Y M N L F I S H E S
P I H A A R J A P O Q U T D K
N G I R O N Y U S B S I A E C
Z A P S T O L L C O E J T E R
E K S O Y I N G K O T U N N I
```

45. ZACCHAEUS

Luke 19:2-10

And, behold, there was a man named Zacchaeus,
which was the ___ ___ ___ ___ ___ among the
___ ___ ___ ___ ___ ___ ___ ___ ___, and he was ___ ___ ___ ___.
3 And he sought to see Jesus who he was; and could not for
the press, because he was ___ ___ ___ ___ ___ ___ of stature.
4 And he ran before, and ___ ___ ___ ___ ___ ___ ___ up into a
___ ___ ___ ___ ___ ___ ___ ___ tree to see him: for he was to
pass that way. 5 And when ___ ___ ___ ___ ___ came to the place,
he looked up, and saw him, and said unto him, Zacchaeus, make
___ ___ ___ ___ ___, and come down; for to day I must abide at thy
___ ___ ___ ___ ___. 6 And he made haste, and came down, and
received him ___ ___ ___ ___ ___ ___ ___ ___. 7 And when they
saw it, they all ___ ___ ___ ___ ___ ___ ___ ___, saying, That he
was gone to be guest with a man that is a ___ ___ ___ ___ ___ ___.
8 And Zacchaeus stood, and said unto the Lord: Behold, Lord, the
half of my goods I give to the ___ ___ ___ ___; and if I have taken
any thing from any man by ___ ___ ___ ___ ___ accusation, I restore
him ___ ___ ___ ___ ___ ___ ___ ___. 9 And Jesus said unto him,
This day is ___ ___ ___ ___ ___ ___ ___ ___ ___ come to this house,
forsomuch as he also is a ___ ___ ___ of ___ ___ ___ ___ ___ ___ ___.
10 For the Son of man is come to ___ ___ ___ ___ and to
___ ___ ___ ___ that which was ___ ___ ___ ___.

```
O Y E S U O H A L C H J E V E
R M A J N R C L I M B E D C K
G O S O N L I N T E A S A U C
C R R Y G E R Y T H D U M G H
A N I F C S T O L S W S M A N
J A E U E O X Q E D O A U S U
N R V L R U M U L A H L R T P
N E S L A F O O S A L V M E K
F N P Y I B F R R K O A U R E
A N R O J R B B O E O T R S I
R I A N U R A E O C H I E F P
E S T O E H T T P S T O D O P
N T F E P U B L I C A N S T D
M E S G O S S A L A I N G C R
H A S T E V A S E E K F E A Y
```

46. PAUL AND SILAS IN PRISON

Acts 16:25-36

And at ___ ___ ___ ___ ___ ___ ___ ___ Paul and Silas
prayed, and ___ ___ ___ ___ praises unto God: and the
prisoners heard them. **26** And suddenly there was a great
___ ___ ___ ___ ___ ___ ___ ___ ___ ___, so that the foundations of
the prison were shaken: and immediately all the ___ ___ ___ ___ ___
were opened, and every one's bands were loosed. **27** And the keeper of
the ___ ___ ___ ___ ___ ___ awaking out of his ___ ___ ___ ___ ___,
and seeing the prison doors ___ ___ ___ ___, he drew out his
___ ___ ___ ___ ___, and would have killed himself, supposing that
the ___ ___ ___ ___ ___ ___ ___ ___ ___ had been fled. **28** But
Paul cried with a loud voice, saying, Do thyself no ___ ___ ___ ___:
for we are all here. **29** Then he called for a light, and sprang in, and
came ___ ___ ___ ___ ___ ___ ___ ___ ___, and fell down before
Paul and Silas, **30** and brought them out, and said, Sirs, what must I
do to be ___ ___ ___ ___ ___? **31** And they said, Believe on the Lord
Jesus ___ ___ ___ ___ ___ ___, and thou shalt be saved, and thy
___ ___ ___ ___ ___. **32** And they spake unto him the word of the
Lord, and to all that were in his house. **33** And he took them the same
hour of the ___ ___ ___ ___ ___, and washed their stripes; and was
___ ___ ___ ___ ___ ___ ___ ___, he and all his, straightway. **34** And
when he had brought them into his house, he set ___ ___ ___ ___
before them, and rejoiced, believing in ___ ___ ___ with all his house.
35 And when it was day, the magistrates sent the serjeants, saying,
Let those men go. **36** And the ___ ___ ___ ___ ___ ___ of the prison
told this saying to Paul, The magistrates have sent to let you go: now
therefore depart, and go in ___ ___ ___ ___ ___.

```
T O N J E I O M A K N C S W B
S K S W T D P R I S O N C J U
I D S D A E E D A B O T P L K
A C L K E Y N N O Y Q R E S C
G W A L M V G J X U I E A P S
A R S H C H A H W S K M C A T
N T T D R O W S O A N B E H H
R E P E E K R N U B N L G A G
A H O Z Q C E Q J B S I R R I
N K N I U R H I E Y N N U M N
D E C T S T O R N K E G P G D
D J K P R S U N I G N X O O I
T Y F A A W S N R S O M O D M
E R E B S T E G K D T R C H A
A J E M M H P P A E S T I O N
```

47. JESUS RAISES LAZARUS FROM THE DEAD

John 11:20-27, 32-35, 41-44

Then Martha, as soon as she heard that Jesus was coming, went and met him: but Mary sat still in the house. **21** Then said __ __ __ __ __ __ unto Jesus, Lord, if thou hadst been here, my brother had not died. **22** But I know, that even now, whatsoever thou wilt ask of __ __ __, God will give it thee. **23** Jesus saith unto her, Thy __ __ __ __ __ __ __ shall rise again. **24** Martha saith unto him, I know that he shall __ __ __ __ again in the resurrection at the last __ __ __. **25** Jesus said unto her, I am the __ __ __ __ __ __ __ __ __ __ __ __, and the life: he that believeth in me, though he were __ __ __ __, yet shall he live: **26** and whosoever liveth and believeth in me shall never die. Believest thou this? **27** She saith unto him, Yea, Lord: I believe that thou art the __ __ __ __ __ __, the Son of God, which should come into the __ __ __ __ __. . . . **32** Then when Mary was come where Jesus was, and saw him, she fell down at his __ __ __ __, saying unto him, Lord, if thou hadst been here, my brother had not __ __ __ __. **33** When Jesus therefore saw her weeping, and the Jews also __ __ __ __ __ __ __ which came with her, he groaned in the __ __ __ __ __ __, and was troubled. **34** And said, Where have ye laid him? They said unto him, Lord, come and see. **35** Jesus __ __ __ __. . . . **41** Then they took away the __ __ __ __ __ from the place where the dead was laid. And Jesus lifted up his eyes, and said, Father, I thank thee that thou hast __ __ __ __ __ me. **42** And I knew that thou hearest me always: but because of the people which stand by I said it, that they may believe that thou hast sent me. **43** And when he thus had spoken, he

```
I L A S T G C D Y D U O G E X
N U F A H R H M B R O T H E R
D Y H T E B R O D E T I I S E
E G E E Q R I H L A Z A R U S
C Z L E U E S I R F H H S P U
S L R F N N T Y O H Y T I T R
T L A G A O O X W T P R Y E R
A E I X U C N E O R I A D Y E
O H U Q U O E S L T D M H O C
N N V H O P D E L S H W E P T
E Y E A I A M R T G C J A G I
X R R N E E H D I O Z C R N O
A C G D E A D M O D E I D I N
A L U D R E Y M N V B H T Z R
T H O M O S S R H O M E P P H
```

cried with a loud voice, __ __ __ __ __ __ __, come forth.
44 And he that was dead came forth, bound __ __ __ __ and foot
with graveclothes: and his __ __ __ __ was bound about with a
napkin. Jesus saith unto them, Loose him, and let him go.

48. THE WOMAN AT THE WELL

John 4:5-7, 9-11, 13-19, 25-26, 28-30

Then cometh [Jesus] to a city of Samaria. . . . **6** Now Jacob's well was
there. __ __ __ __ __ therefore, being wearied with his journey,
sat thus on the well: and it was about the sixth hour. **7** There cometh a
__ __ __ __ __ of Samaria to draw __ __ __ __ __: Jesus
saith unto her, Give me to __ __ __ __ __. . . . **9** Then saith the
woman of __ __ __ __ __ __ __ unto him, How is it that
thou, being a __ __ __, askest drink of me, which am a woman of
Samaria? for the Jews have no dealings with the Samaritans. **10** Jesus
answered and said unto her, If thou knewest the __ __ __ __
__ __ __ __ __ (3w), and who it is that saith to thee, Give
me to drink; thou wouldest have asked of him, and he would have
given thee __ __ __ __ __ __ water. **11** The woman saith unto
him, Sir, thou hast nothing to __ __ __ __ with, and the well
is deep: from whence then hast thou that living water? . . . **13** Jesus
answered and said unto her, Whosoever drinketh of this water shall
thirst again: **14** but whosoever drinketh of the water that I shall give
him shall never __ __ __ __ __ __; but the water that I shall
give him shall be in him a __ __ __ __ of water springing up
into everlasting __ __ __ __. **15** The woman saith unto him, Sir,
give me this water, that I thirst not, neither come hither to draw.
16 Jesus saith unto her, Go, call thy __ __ __ __ __ __ __ __,
and come hither. **17** The woman __ __ __ __ __ __ __ __
and said, I have no husband. Jesus said unto her, Thou hast well said,
I have no husband: **18** for thou hast had __ __ __ __ husbands;
and he whom thou now hast is not thy husband: in that saidst thou
__ __ __ __ __. **19** The woman saith unto him, Sir, I perceive that
thou art a __ __ __ __ __ __ __. . . . **25** I know that Messias

```
O U D C U O O E M K I N D B O
D K N W T R A Z W I J A C K W
N S D O K S A T T E X M M U H
E B T M M D R A W A T E R R I
A A R A A D B I N N Z A N Y Y
H A D N A B S U H K U I L Y O
E I O Z N H O L S T P U I L B
K R G I S N I Q M H R F V S E
N A F M W F B U N T O X I M P
I M O D E S O X Y L P E N R P
W A T E R P O T D B H D G Z A
E S F H E V I F R J E S U S C
L G I B D C H R I S T Q M A S
L B G M E L X I N V T U I N G
R D N M I A F E K R E B B Y G
```

cometh, which is called ___ ___ ___ ___ ___ ___: when he is come, he
will tell us all things. **26** Jesus saith unto her, I that speak unto thee am
he. . . . **28** The woman then left her ___ ___ ___ ___ ___ ___ ___ ___,
and went her way into the ___ ___ ___ ___, and saith to the men,
29 Come, see a man, which told me all things that ever I did: is not this
the Christ? **30** Then they went out of the city, and came unto him.

49. JESUS CALMS THE STORM

Mark 4:35-41

35 And the same day, when the even was come, he saith unto them, Let us pass over unto the other ___ ___ ___ ___. **36** And when they had sent away the ___ ___ ___ ___ ___ ___ ___ ___ ___, they took him even as he was in the _ _ _ _. And there were also with him other ___ ___ ___ ___ ___ ___ ships. **37** And there arose a great storm of wind, and the ___ ___ ___ ___ ___ beat into the ship, so that it was now ___ ___ ___ ___. **38** And he was in the hinder part of the ship, asleep on a ___ ___ ___ ___ ___ ___: and they awake him, and say unto him, ___ ___ ___ ___ ___ ___, carest thou not that we ___ ___ ___ ___ ___ ___? **39** And he arose, and rebuked the ___ ___ ___ ___, and said unto the sea, ___ ___ ___ ___ ___, be ___ ___ ___ ___ ___. And the wind ceased, and there was a great ___ ___ ___ ___. **40** And he ___ ___ ___ ___ unto them, Why are ye so ___ ___ ___ ___ ___ ___ ___? how is it that ye have no ___ ___ ___ ___ ___? **41** And they feared exceedingly, and said one to ___ ___ ___ ___ ___ ___ ___, What ___ ___ ___ ___ ___ ___ of man is this, that even the wind and the ___ ___ ___ obey him?

```
A P C C O O R E N N A M W A B
T W A T T P O P A K Y U B R O
F U L L P C L D I A G L E T P
K O M U I J L P A H E T C I U
C A Y F L T I P W O S I D E R
E H E R L Q T M S A A T X T F
K A F A O U S L M B I U Y H K
O P N E W H N N E S D D R U C
R N Y F A I T H S I R E P T P
I W T O V O W V H G H I H S C
P Y R B E X P F N T F O Y G T
Y J A E S K U D O M M O P G I
T Y S H O W I N D T I W O Y O
A O O T P E A C E W A R V K N
V P E T R K E D D G I B B E A
```

50. PETER WALKS ON WATER

Matthew 14:22-33

22 And straightway Jesus constrained his
__ __ __ __ __ __ __ __ __ to get into a ship, and to
go before him unto the other side, while he sent the multitudes
away. **23** And when he had sent the multitudes away, he went
up into a mountain apart to __ __ __ __: and when the
evening was come, he was there __ __ __ __ __. **24** But
the ship was now in the midst of the __ __ __, tossed with
__ __ __ __ __: for the wind was contrary. **25** And in the
fourth watch of the __ __ __ __ __ Jesus went unto them,
__ __ __ __ __ __ __ on the sea. **26** And when the disciples
saw him walking on the sea, they were troubled, saying, It is a
__ __ __ __ __ __; and they cried out for __ __ __ __.
27 But straightway Jesus spake unto them, saying, Be of good
__ __ __ __ __; it is I; be not __ __ __ __ __ __.
28 And Peter answered him and said, Lord, if it be thou, bid
me come unto thee on the __ __ __ __ __. **29** And he
said, Come. And when __ __ __ __ __ was come down
out of the __ __ __ __, he walked on the water, to go to
__ __ __ __ __. **30** But when he saw the wind boisterous,
he was afraid; and beginning to __ __ __ __, he cried, saying,
Lord, __ __ __ __ __ __ (2w). **31** And immediately Jesus
stretched forth his __ __ __ __, and caught him, and said
unto him, O thou of little __ __ __ __ __, wherefore didst
thou __ __ __ __ __? **32** And when they were come into the
ship, the wind ceased. **33** Then they that were in the ship came and
__ __ __ __ __ __ __ __ __ him, saying, Of a truth
thou art the __ __ __ __ __ __ __ __ (3w).

```
N K J S O N O F G O D B P A G
G T E W P E E W G S O S K R O
N E S K T D E P P I H S R O W
I R J L L I O P D B T A C P A
D L E G U S T U D Y I W N E T
L O S T Y C K S B R A J E D E
P H U G E I Y C P T F L E K R
P L S N N P R A Y Q U L O C S
A J C W A L K I N G J S S N F
E E S A O E J U I P F D D O E
S T S V O S I C G D I A R F A
G I Y E P B N S H E C H E E R
S O E S P I R I T S L L S N R
L N E D G C U N D S K E E N S
S A V E M E Q K E P P C Y A E
```

ANSWERS

1

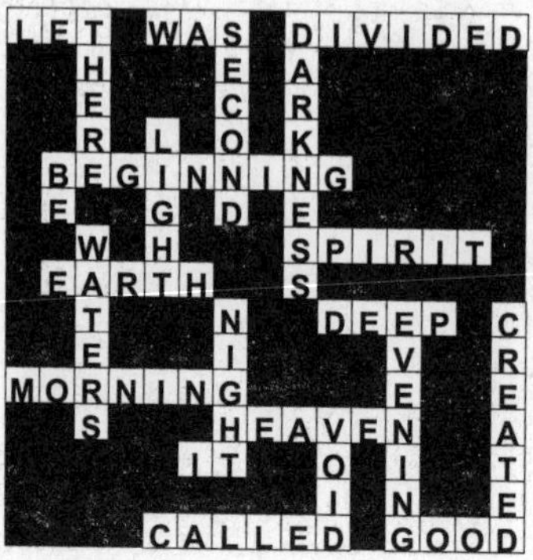

2

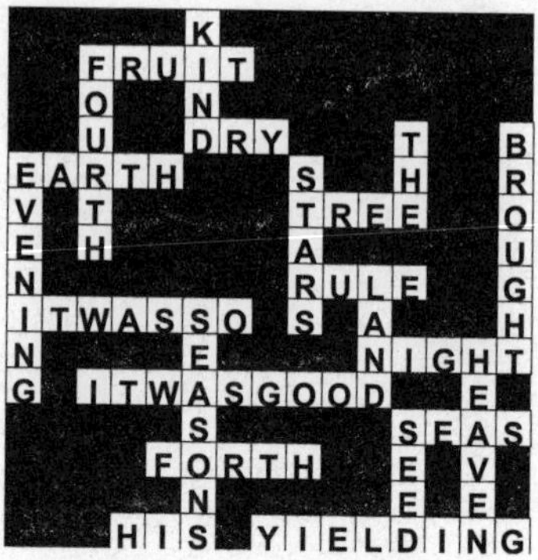

3

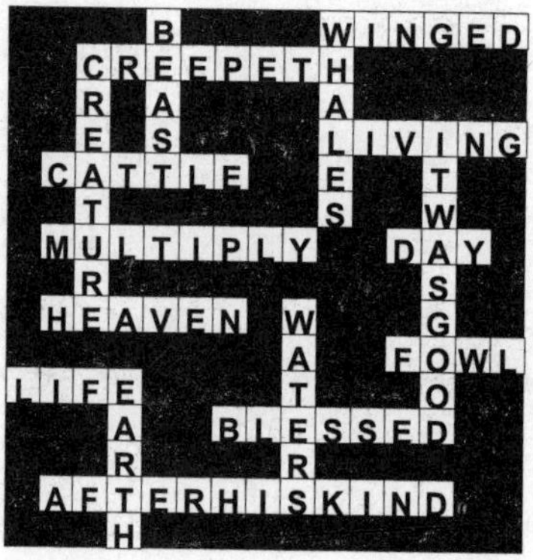

4

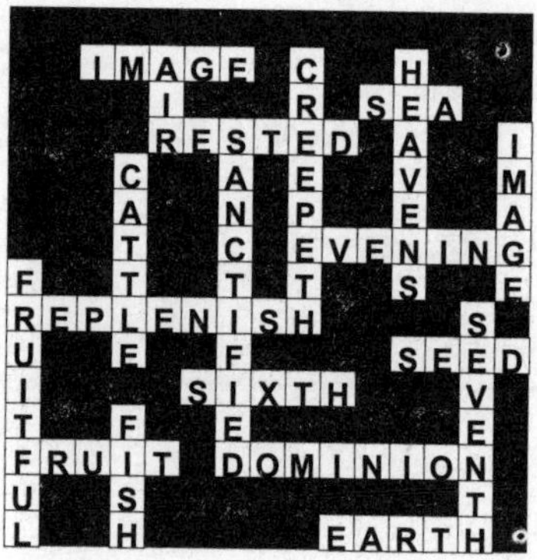

5

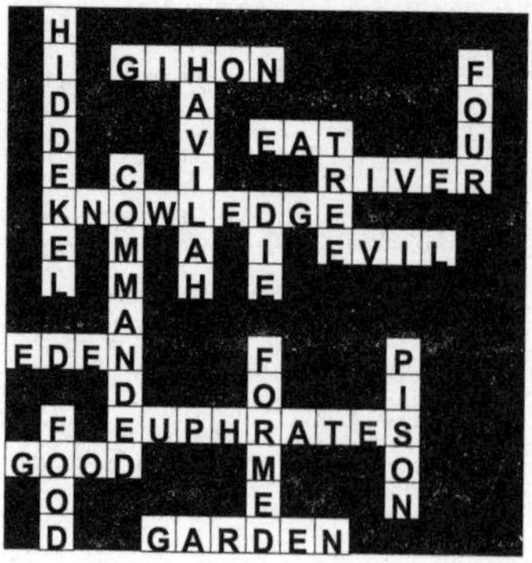

6

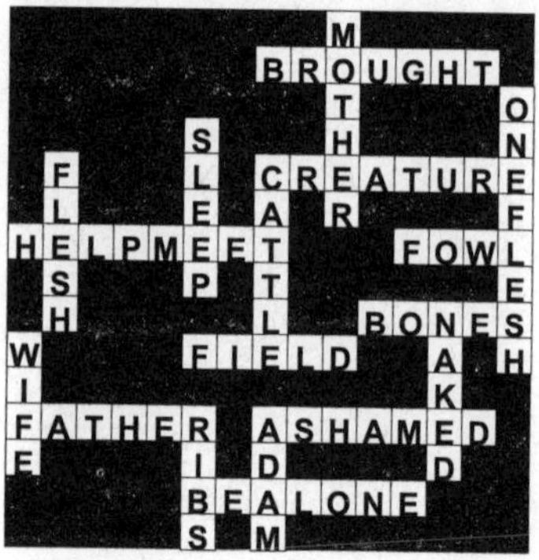

ANSWERS

7

8

9

10

11

12

ANSWERS

13

14

15

16

17

18

ANSWERS

19

20

21

22

23

24

ANSWERS

25

26

27

28

29

30

ANSWERS

31

32

33

34

35

36

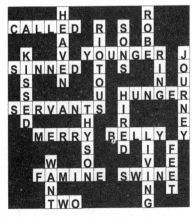

ANSWERS

37

38

39

40

41

42

ANSWERS

43

44

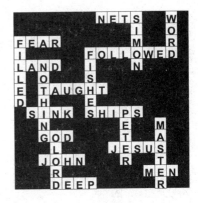

45

46

47

48

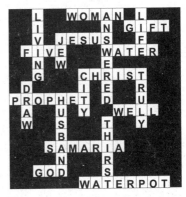

ANSWERS

49

50

ANSWERS

1

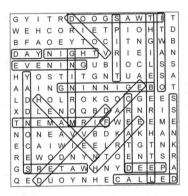

2

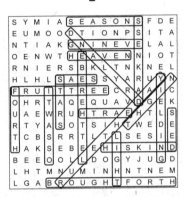

3

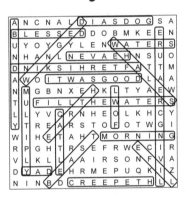

4

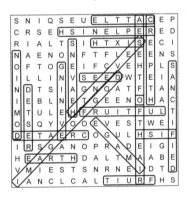

5

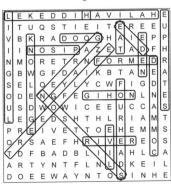

6

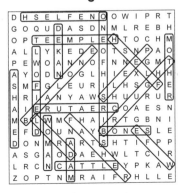

ANSWERS

7

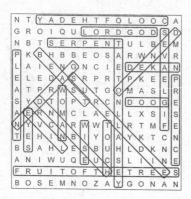

8

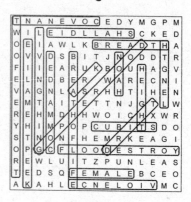

9

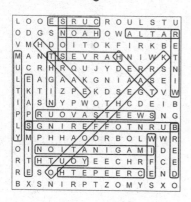

10

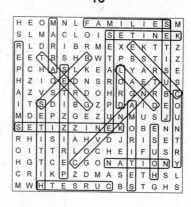

11

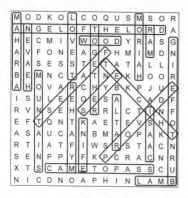

12

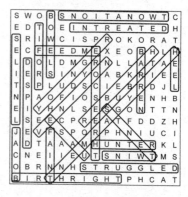

ANSWERS

13

```
I H O U S E O F L E V I C S O
O D W G F L E S R E H H S A W
D H R R A S T D Y H P A C O R
G T I E T N M L W E C O H S P
M I H W E R D I T S M O I C H
A D C M R O E H E P U S L D E
I E S T A O L L C A S T D A U
D S I G W E A S G E O Y R I U
S C R P A E R S J R S A T E G W
C U H Y U I P H A C K I N H E
E N A Q O L S E G A W Y H T
S I R N O S R E H E M A C E B
S G A B O A D Z F F Y N S R E
O H O N B U L R U S H E S M H
M T H R E E M O N T H S D O X
```

14

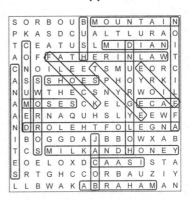

```
S O R B O U B M O U N T A I N
P K A S D C U A L T L U R A O
T C E A T U S L M I D I A N I
A O F F A T H E R I N L A W T
C N O I L E E T S M U E O R C
A S S S H O E S P H O Y R K I
N U W T H E C S N Y R W O I L
E R M O S E S C K E L G E C A F
A R N A Q U H S L Y E E W F
N D R O L E H T F O L E G N A
I B O G G D A J B B O W X A B
T C S M I L K A N D H O N E Y
E O E L O X D C A A S I S T A
S R T G H C C O R B A U Z I Y
L L B W A K A B R A H A M A N
```

15

```
G Y B S I R L O G F A I N G D
G D E R E V O C D N A L Y R D
D O L A O R M I S R A E L O N
N O I P S A V E D O B E H U I
C M E Z Y I S L N Y F O E N W
H R V S D P S P A T A V B D T
A X E N Q U A H R W E P I S
R S D A G E S G A T U R G D A
I E S S B Y H R T H T C K E
O T H X R P P H K C H Y M C
T O V O R Q U T F E A R E D K
S M O R N I N G I R E E N F A
R M N E A Q U H D A F W R B L
A G H R A I N A Z T N C H U T
B T G L L Z G N E M E S R O H
```

16

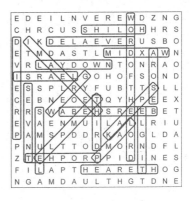

```
E D E I L N V E R E W D Z N G
C H R C U S S H I L O H H R S
D I K D E L A E V E R U S B O
E T M D A S T L M I D X A W
V R L A Y D O W N T O N R A O
I S R A E L G O H O F S O N D
E S S P L R Y F U B T S L L
C E B N E O E T Q Y H P E E X
R R S W A B E H S R E E B E T
E V A E N M U I L A L R I U
P A M S P D D R K A O G L D A
N U L T T O D M O R N D F L
Z T E H P O R P P I D I N E S
F I L A P T H E A R E T H O G
N G A M D A U L T H G T D N E
```

17

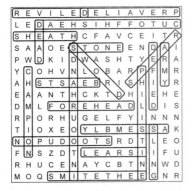

```
R E V I L E D E L I A V E R P
L E D A E H S I H F F O T U C
S H E A T H C F A V C E I T R
S A A O E S T O N E N D A I
P W D K I D W A S H T Y E R A
Y C O H V N L O B A R P F M R
A H S T S A E B R I S H I I Y
E A A N T H C K T D H I E H E
D M L F O R E H E A D L D I S
R P O R H U G E L F Y I N N H
T I O X E O Y L B M E S S A K
N O P U D O O T S R D T L E O
F N S Z D T L E A R S I I F U
R H U C E N A Y C B T N N W D
M O Q S M I T E T H E E G N R
```

18

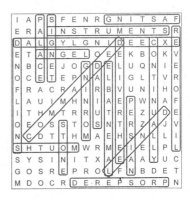

```
I A P S F E N R G N I T S A F
E R A I N S T R U M E N T S R
D A L G Y L G N I D E E C X E
E T A N G E L O E E K B O K V
N B C E J O G E L U Q N I E
O C E T E P N A L I G L T V R
F R A C R A I R B V U N I H O
L A U I M H N I A E P W N A F
I T H M T R R U T R E Z U D E
O E O S T O S N A E H S N L L
N C D T T H M A E H S N L P L
S H T U O M W R M E I E L P L
S Y S I N I T X A E A Y U C
G O S R E P R O L F N B D E T
M D O C R D E R E P S O R P N
```

ANSWERS

19

```
C I F S S A P O T E M A C Y H
S Y E H B J I C K T W E H T U
K U N I A U E C T X I L I T N
E F E N L P I R P E O P L E D
W A G A S R B L E D L E D N E
K C L R B K F A D A E R R E R
L E I O P A D Y N N B S E H R
P H V T T E N G E O A R N T T
A L N N Y N U W H T B E X R A
C K A R P A O R S H S W F A N
H I S H G L F I R E E A M E D
D D N E M U N L E R S N E I T
I S E I K Q O H E A V E N T I
H C E E P S C A T T E R E D S
N T D E N I G A M I M E I M F
```

20

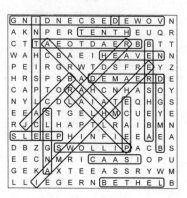

21

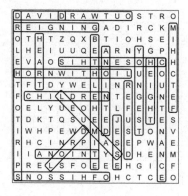

22

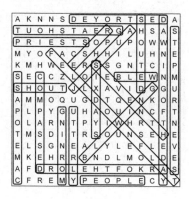

23

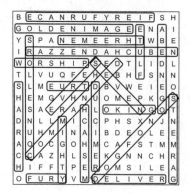

24

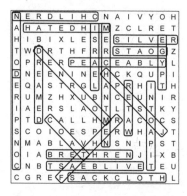

ANSWERS

25

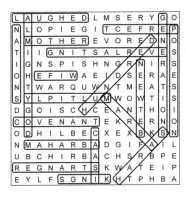

26

27

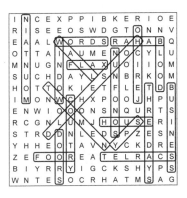

28

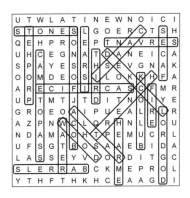

29

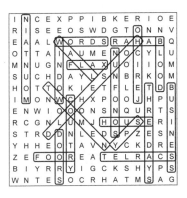

30

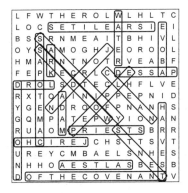

ANSWERS

31

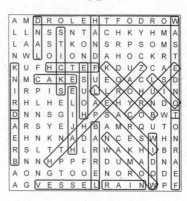

32

33

34

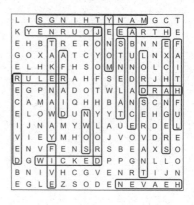

35

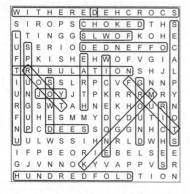

36

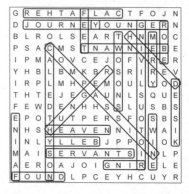

ANSWERS

37

```
C A T G N I L B M E R T H V O
H K S O M E B O D Y S G E Y L
C E N R A I E S C R S W L E G
L S A S N U T R N O C H O P T
E A H I S T L E P N L H O H P S
A X C R L M S H O G V T W I T
N W I S S U E O F B L O O D R A
S V S G G A R M E N T U M A A
E O Y Q M Y D E Q U J C A U N
D I H U M W E L T K C H N G G
E C P R I E S T S S K E N H E
L E P E R S C E P P A D G T R
A S T I O N I G N I Z M H E K
E O L J D D G A L I L E E R L
H T I A F V O M A X N N N J A
```

38

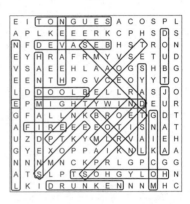

39

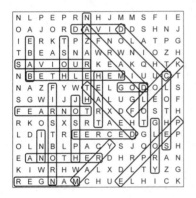

40

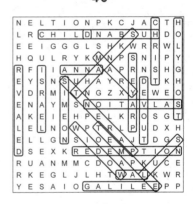

41

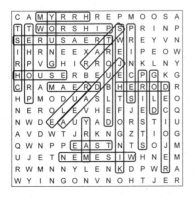

42

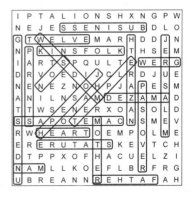

43

```
P I N R A L A W E E J U P A Y
L W C Y W I J Z K R E L U R J
L B E L I E V E D E A Y R E L
R X M B S N Q W E N E E I B X
G M K U O I Y U A E H O F Y U
Y C S E X W D C R T J O Y B E
S S T I C H O G O W E B I I E
Y R O L G T I M I S H R N N K
I J N I I Y T A A T Q I G F F
N F E A S T N R C N U M K O W
G L L E X N S R E A R N T O T
E C H S K A J I H V U S C K I
K R E H W C H A X R T H B T O
R O N R E V O G D E Z B J Y N
W M I R A C L E S S W O U O H
```

44

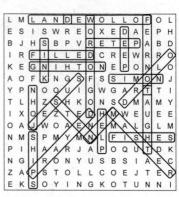

```
L M L A N D E W O L L O F O L
E S I S W R E O X E D A E P H
B J H S B P V R E T E P A B D
I R F I L L E D C R E W R R O
K E G N I H T O N E P O N L O
A O F K N G S F S I M O N J
Y P N O O U I G W G A R T T I
T L H Z S H K O N S D M A M Y
I X O E Z T E D H M W E U E E
O A J W O A E N E M A L G L M
N M S P M Y M N L F I S H E S
P I H A A R J A P O Q U T D K
Z A P S T O L L C O E J T E R
E K S O Y I N G K O T U N N I
```

45

```
O Y E S U O H A L C H J E V E
R M A J N R C L I M B E D C K
G O S O N L I N T E A S A U C
C R R Y G E R Y T H D U M G H
A N I F C S T O L S W S M A N
J A E U E O X Q E D O A U S U
N R V L R U M U L A H L R T P
N E S L A F O O S A L V M E K
F N P Y I B F R R K O A U R E
A N R O J R B B O E O T R S I
R I A N U R A E O C H I E F P
E S T O E H T T P S T O D O P
N T F E P U B L I C A N S T D
M E S G O S S A L A I N G C R
H A S T E V A S E E K F E A Y
```

46

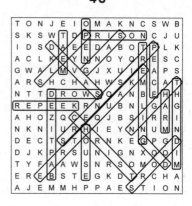

```
T O N J E I O M A K N C S W B
S K S W T D P R I S O N C J U
I D S D A E E D A B O T P L K
A C L K E Y N N O Y O R E S C
G W A L M V G J X U I E A P S
A R S H C H A W S K M C A T
N T T D R O W S O A N B E H H
R E P E E K R N U B N L G A G
A H O Z Q C E Q J B S I R R I
N K N I U R H I E Y N N U M N
D E C T S T O R N K E G P G D
D J K P R S U N I G N X O O I
T Y F A A W S N R S O M O D M
E R E B S T E G K D T R C H A
A J E M M H P P A E S T I O N
```

47

```
I L A S T G C D Y D U O G E X
N U F A H R H M B R O T H E R
D Y H T E B R O D E T I I S E
E G E E Q R I H L A Z A R U S
C Z L E U E S I R F H H S P U
S L R F N N T Y O H Y T I T R
T L A G A O X W T P R Y E R
A E I X U C N E O R I A D Y E
O H U Q U O E S L T D M H O C
N N V H O P D E L S H W E P T
E Y E A I A M R T G C J A G I
X R R N E E H D I O Z C R N O
A C G D E A D M O D E I D I N
A L U D R E Y M N V B H T Z R
T H O M O S S R H O M E P P H
```

48

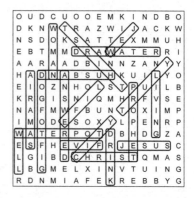

```
O U D C U O O E M K I N D B O
D K N W T R A Z W I J A C K W
N S D O K S A T T E X M M U H
E B T M M D R A W A T E R R I
A A R A A D B I N N Z A N Y Y
H A D N A B S U H K U I L Y O
E I O Z N H O L S T P U I L B
K R G I S N I Q M H R F V S E
N A F M W F B U N T O X I M P
I M O D E S O X Y L P E N R P
W A T E R P O T D B H D G Z A
E S F H E V I F R J E S U S C
L G I B D C H R I S T Q M A S
L B G M E L X I N V T U I N G
R D N M I A F E K R E B B Y G
```

ANSWERS

49

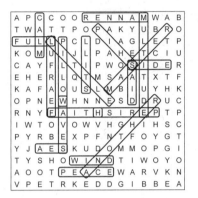

50

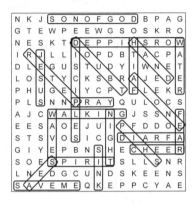

MORE GREAT BIBLE PUZZLES!

Here's a fun collection of 100 Bible word searches with a bonus—
"hidden trivia" questions made from the leftover letters! These 100
puzzles are based on the beloved King James Version and cover the
gamut of scripture—from Genesis to Revelation, including the
people, places, things, and ideas of God's Word.

Paperback / 978-1-63609-715-2